PowerPoint 2003: Advanced

Student Manual

Instructor Joan Farougi   10/23/07

Australia • Canada • Mexico • Singapore
Spain • United Kingdom • United States

PowerPoint 2003: Advanced

VP and GM of Courseware:	Michael Springer
Series Product Managers:	Adam A. Wilcox and Charles G. Blum
Developmental Editor:	Jim O'Shea and Leslie Caico
Keytester:	Bill Bateman
Series Designer:	Adam A. Wilcox
Cover Designer:	Abby Scholz

COPYRIGHT © 2006 Course Technology, a division of Thomson Learning. Thomson Learning is a trademark used herein under license.

ALL RIGHTS RESERVED. No part of this work may be reproduced, transcribed, or used in any form or by any means—graphic, electronic, or mechanical, including photocopying, recording, taping, Web distribution, or information storage and retrieval systems—without the prior written permission of the publisher.

For more information contact:

Course Technology
25 Thomson Place
Boston, MA 02210

Or find us on the Web at: www.course.com

For permission to use material from this text or product, submit a request online at: www.thomsonrights.com

Any additional questions about permissions can be submitted by e-mail to: thomsonrights@thomson.com

Trademarks

Course ILT is a trademark of Course Technology.

Some of the product names and company names used in this book have been used for identification purposes only and may be trademarks or registered trademarks of their respective manufacturers and sellers.

Disclaimers

Course Technology reserves the right to revise this publication and make changes from time to time in its content without notice.

*The ProCert Labs numerical rating referenced is based on an independent review of this instructional material and is a separate analysis independent of Certiport or the Microsoft Office Specialist program.

Microsoft, the Office Logo, Outlook, and PowerPoint are either registered trademarks or trademarks of Microsoft Corporation in the United States and/or other countries. The Microsoft Office Specialist Logo is used under license from owner.

Certiport and the Certiport Approved Courseware logo are registered trademarks of Certiport Inc. in the United States and/or other countries.

Course Technology is independent from Microsoft Corporation or Certiport, and not affiliated with Microsoft or Certiport in any manner. While this publication may be used in assisting individuals to prepare for a Microsoft Office Specialist exam, Microsoft, Certiport, and Course Technology do not warrant that use of this publication will ensure passing a Microsoft Office Specialist exam.

ISBNs

ISBN-13: 978-1-4188-8949-4 = Student Manual
ISBN-10: 1-4188-8949-0 = Student Manual

ISBN-13: 978-1-4188-8951-7 = Student Manual with CDs (student data and CBT)
ISBN-10: 1-4188-8951-2 = Student Manual with CDs (student data and CBT)

Printed in the United States of America

3 4 5 6 7 8 9 PM 08 07

What does the Microsoft Office Specialist Approved Courseware logo represent?

Only the finest courseware receives approval to bear the Microsoft® Office Specialist logo. In order to give candidates the greatest chance of success at becoming a Microsoft® Office Specialist, all approved courseware has been reviewed by an independent third party for quality of content and adherence to exam objectives. This specific course has been mapped to the following Microsoft® Office Specialist Exam Skill Standards:

- PowerPoint 2003 Specialist

What is Microsoft Office Specialist certification?

Microsoft Office Specialist certification shows that employees, candidates and students have something exceptional to offer—proven expertise in Microsoft Office programs. Recognized by businesses and schools around the world, it is the only Microsoft-approved certification program of its kind. There are four levels of certification available: Specialist, Expert, Master, and Master Instructor.[1] Certification is available for the following Microsoft Office programs:

- Microsoft Word
- Microsoft PowerPoint®
- Microsoft Excel
- Microsoft Outlook®
- Microsoft Access
- Microsoft Project

For more information

To learn more about becoming a Microsoft Office Specialist, visit www.microsoft.com/officespecialist.

To learn about other Microsoft Office Specialist approved courseware from Course Technology, visit www.course.com.

---

[1] The availability of Microsoft Office Specialist certification exams varies by Microsoft Office program, program version, and language. Visit www.microsoft.com/officespecialist for exam availability.

Contents

Introduction iii
Topic A: About the manual...iv
Topic B: Setting your expectations...viii
Topic C: Re-keying the course xii

Building custom presentations 1-1
Topic A: Modifying templates..1-2
Topic B: Building custom templates 1-4
Topic C: Building custom slide masters 1-8
Topic D: Advanced slide master techniques...1-13
Unit summary: Building custom presentations 1-18

Using multimedia in presentations 2-1
Topic A: Advanced clip art and drawing techniques................................2-2
Topic B: Adding movies and sound 2-10
Topic C: Using animations 2-12
Topic D: Using scanned images..2-17
Unit summary: Using multimedia in presentations................................2-18

Using organization charts and tables 3-1
Topic A: Advanced organization chart options 3-2
Topic B: Formatting and modifying tables...3-9
Unit summary: Using organization charts and tables.............................3-16

Advanced presentation techniques 4-1
Topic A: Adding special effects..4-2
Topic B: Working with slide show options 4-6
Topic C: Setting up review cycles 4-8
Unit summary: Advanced presentation techniques 4-13

Advanced presentation delivery options 5-1
Topic A: Online meetings...5-2
Topic B: Working with shared workspaces 5-5
Topic C: Working with the Package for CD feature...............................5-10
Topic D: Advanced delivery techniques...5-16
Unit summary: Advanced presentation delivery options 5-21

Customizing the environment 6-1
Topic A: Customizing and creating toolbars 6-2
Topic B: Automating your work...6-8
Unit summary: Customizing the environment 6-11

Microsoft Office integration 7-1
Topic A: Working with Excel...7-2
Topic B: Working with Word...7-8
Unit summary: Microsoft Office integration...7-17

Microsoft Office Specialist exam objectives map   **A-1**
   Topic A: Comprehensive exam objectives A-2

Course summary   **S-1**
   Topic A: Course summary S-2
   Topic B: Continued learning after class S-4

Quick reference   **Q-1**

Glossary   **G-1**

Index   **I-1**

Introduction

After reading this introduction, you will know how to:

A Use Course Technology ILT manuals in general.

B Use prerequisites, a target student description, course objectives, and a skills inventory to properly set your expectations for the course.

C Re-key this course after class.

Topic A: About the manual

Course Technology ILT philosophy

Course Technology ILT manuals facilitate your learning by providing structured interaction with the software itself. While we provide text to explain difficult concepts, the hands-on activities are the focus of our courses. By paying close attention as your instructor leads you through these activities, you will learn the skills and concepts effectively.

We believe strongly in the instructor-led classroom. During class, focus on your instructor. Our manuals are designed and written to facilitate your interaction with your instructor, and not to call attention to manuals themselves.

We believe in the basic approach of setting expectations, delivering instruction, and providing summary and review afterwards. For this reason, lessons begin with objectives and end with summaries. We also provide overall course objectives and a course summary to provide both an introduction to and closure on the entire course.

Manual components

The manuals contain these major components:

- Table of contents
- Introduction
- Units
- Appendix
- Course summary
- Quick reference
- Glossary
- Index

Each element is described below.

Table of contents

The table of contents acts as a learning roadmap.

Introduction

The introduction contains information about our training philosophy and our manual components, features, and conventions. It contains target student, prerequisite, objective, and setup information for the specific course.

Units

Units are the largest structural component of the course content. A unit begins with a title page that lists objectives for each major subdivision, or topic, within the unit. Within each topic, conceptual and explanatory information alternates with hands-on activities. Units conclude with a summary comprising one paragraph for each topic, and an independent practice activity that gives you an opportunity to practice the skills you've learned.

The conceptual information takes the form of text paragraphs, exhibits, lists, and tables. The activities are structured in two columns, one telling you what to do, the other providing explanations, descriptions, and graphics.

Appendix

The appendix for this course lists the Microsoft Office Specialist exam objectives for PowerPoint 2003 along with references to corresponding coverage in Course ILT courseware.

Course summary

This section provides a text summary of the entire course. It is useful for providing closure at the end of the course. The course summary also indicates the next course in this series, if there is one, and lists additional resources you might find useful as you continue to learn about the software.

Quick reference

The quick reference is an at-a-glance job aid summarizing some of the more common features of the software.

Glossary

The glossary provides definitions for all of the key terms used in this course.

Index

The index at the end of this manual makes it easy for you to find information about a particular software component, feature, or concept.

Manual conventions

We've tried to keep the number of elements and the types of formatting to a minimum in the manuals. This aids in clarity and makes the manuals more classically elegant looking. But there are some conventions and icons you should know about.

Convention	Description
Italic text	In conceptual text, indicates a new term or feature.
Bold text	In unit summaries, indicates a key term or concept. In an independent practice activity, indicates an explicit item that you select, choose, or type.
`Code font`	Indicates code or syntax.
`Longer strings of ▶ code will look ▶ like this.`	In the hands-on activities, any code that's too long to fit on a single line is divided into segments by one or more continuation characters (▶). This code should be entered as a continuous string of text.
Select **bold item**	In the left column of hands-on activities, bold sans-serif text indicates an explicit item that you select, choose, or type.
Keycaps like ⏎ ENTER	Indicate a key on the keyboard you must press.

Hands-on activities

The hands-on activities are the most important parts of our manuals. They are divided into two primary columns. The "Here's how" column gives short instructions to you about what to do. The "Here's why" column provides explanations, graphics, and clarifications. Here's a sample:

Do it!

A-1: Creating a commission formula

Here's how	Here's why
1 Open Sales	This is an oversimplified sales compensation worksheet. It shows sales totals, commissions, and incentives for five sales reps.
2 Observe the contents of cell F4	F4 = =E4*C_Rate
	The commission rate formulas use the name "C_Rate" instead of a value for the commission rate.

For these activities, we have provided a collection of data files designed to help you learn each skill in a real-world business context. As you work through the activities, you will modify and update these files. Of course, you might make a mistake and, therefore, want to re-key the activity starting from scratch. To make it easy to start over, you will rename each data file at the end of the first activity in which the file is modified. Our convention for renaming files is to add the word "My" to the beginning of the file name. In the above activity, for example, a file called "Sales" is being used for the first time. At the end of this activity, you would save the file as "My sales," thus leaving the "Sales" file unchanged. If you make a mistake, you can start over using the original "Sales" file.

In some activities, however, it may not be practical to rename the data file. If you want to retry one of these activities, ask your instructor for a fresh copy of the original data file.

Topic B: Setting your expectations

Properly setting your expectations is essential to your success. This topic will help you do that by providing:

- Prerequisites for this course
- A description of the target student at whom the course is aimed
- A list of the objectives for the course
- A skills assessment for the course

Course prerequisites

Before taking this course, you should be familiar with personal computers and the use of a keyboard and a mouse. Furthermore, this course assumes that you've completed the following courses or have equivalent experience:

- *PowerPoint 2003: Basic*

Target student

You should be comfortable using a personal computer and Windows 2000 or Windows XP. You also need to know the basics of using PowerPoint 2003. You'll get the most out of this course if your goal is to become proficient using PowerPoint's advanced features to create enhanced presentations.

Microsoft Office Specialist certification

This course is designed to help you pass the Microsoft Office Specialist exam for PowerPoint 2003. For complete certification training, you should complete both this course and *PowerPoint 2003: Basic*.

Course objectives

These overall course objectives will give you an idea about what to expect from the course. It is also possible that they will help you see that this course is not the right one for you. If you think you either lack the prerequisite knowledge or already know most of the subject matter to be covered, you should let your instructor know that you think you are misplaced in the class.

Note: In addition to the general objectives listed below, specific Microsoft Office Specialist exam objectives are listed at the beginning of each topic. For a complete mapping of exam objectives to Course ILT content, see Appendix A.

After completing this course, you will know how to:

- Modify a template; create a template from a blank presentation, and add graphic elements to it; build a custom slide master; and work with slide masters.
- Work with advanced clip art and drawing techniques; and add sound clips, movie clips, animation effects, and scanned images to a presentation.
- Use advanced organization-chart options; format tables; and draw tables in a presentation.
- Add and modify action buttons; create and edit custom slide shows; and set up a review cycle.

- Use Microsoft NetMeeting to broadcast a presentation on demand; work with shared workspaces; embed fonts and compress pictures; use the Package for CD feature; run a packaged presentation; and use advanced delivery techniques.
- Customize a toolbar; create a toolbar; and create and run a macro.
- Insert and edit an Excel worksheet; build slides from a Word outline; insert a Word table into a presentation; send a presentation to Word; edit a presentation in Word; and save a presentation as an RTF outline.

Skills inventory

Use the following form to gauge your skill level entering the class. For each skill listed, rate your familiarity from 1 to 5, with five being the most familiar. *This is not a test.* Rather, it is intended to provide you with an idea of where you're starting from at the beginning of class. If you're wholly unfamiliar with all the skills, you might not be ready for the class. If you think you already understand all of the skills, you might need to move on to the next course in the series. In either case, you should let your instructor know as soon as possible.

Skill	1	2	3	4	5
Modifying templates					
Creating a custom template from a blank presentation					
Building custom slide masters					
Working with slide masters					
Formatting and rotating objects					
Adding sound and movie clips					
Adding scanned images and animation effects					
Formatting organization charts and tables					
Adding and modifying action buttons					
Creating and editing custom slide shows					
Setting up a review cycle					
Using Microsoft NetMeeting					
Working with shared workspace					
Embedding fonts in a presentation					
Compressing pictures to reduce the size of a presentation					
Packaging and running a presentation					
Using on-screen navigation tools, and annotating a slide					
Customizing and creating toolbars					

Skill	1	2	3	4	5
Creating and running a macro					
Embedding and editing Excel worksheets					
Building slides from a Word outline					
Inserting Word tables into a presentation					
Sending a presentation to Word					
Editing a presentation in Word					
Saving a presentation as an RTF outline					

Topic C: Re-keying the course

If you have the proper hardware and software, you can re-key this course after class. This section explains what you'll need in order to do so, and how to do it.

Computer requirements

To re-key this course, your personal computer must have:

- A keyboard and a mouse
- Pentium 233 MHz processor (or higher)
- 128 MB RAM
- 400 MB available hard disk space
- CD-ROM drive
- SVGA monitor (800×600 minimum resolution support)
- A sound card and speakers, if you want to complete the multimedia activities in Units 2 and 4
- Internet access, if you'll be downloading the Student Data files from www.courseilt.com, and for installing the latest service packs and security patches from www.windowsupdate.com

Setup instructions to re-key the course

Before you re-key the course, you will need to perform the following steps.

1. Install Microsoft Windows 2000 Professional on an NTFS partition according to the software manufacturer's instructions. Then, install the latest critical updates and service packs from www.windowsupdate.com. (You can also use Windows XP Professional, although the screen shots in this course were taken using Windows 2000, so your screens might look somewhat different.)
2. Adjust your computer's display properties as follows:
   a. Open the Control Panel and double-click Display to open the Display Properties dialog box.
   b. On the Settings tab, change the Colors setting to True Color (24 bit or 32 bit) and the Screen area to 800 by 600 pixels.
   c. On the Appearance tab, set the Scheme to Windows Classic.
   d. Click OK. If you are prompted to accept the new settings, click OK and click Yes. Then, if necessary, close the Display Properties dialog box.
3. Adjust your computer's Internet settings as follows:
   a. On the desktop, right-click the Internet Explorer icon and choose Properties to open the Internet Properties dialog box.
   b. On the Connections tab, click Setup to start the Internet Connection Wizard.
   c. Click Cancel. A message box will appear.
   d. Check "Do not show the Internet Connection wizard in the future" and click Yes.
   e. Re-open the Internet Properties dialog box.
   f. On the General tab, click Use Blank, click Apply, and click OK.

4　If you want to complete the multimedia activities in Units 2 and 4, you'll need speakers, a sound card, and a sound driver. To install a sound driver, use the disk provided by the manufacturer.

5　Install Microsoft Office 2003 according to the software manufacturer's instructions, as follows:

    a　When prompted for the CD key, enter the 25-character code included with your software.

    b　Select the Custom installation option and click Next.

    c　Clear the check box next to Access.

    d　Select "Choose advanced customization of applications" and click Next.

    e　Next to Microsoft Office PowerPoint for Windows, click the drop-down arrow and choose Run all from My Computer.

    f　Click the plus sign (+) next to Office Shared Features. Then, next to Converters and Filters, click the drop-down arrow and choose Run all from My Computer.

    g　Click Next. Then, click Install to start the installation.

    h　When the installation has completed successfully, click Finish.

6　Start PowerPoint. Then, turn off the Office Assistant, as follows:

    a　If the Office Assistant is not displayed, choose Help, Show the Office Assistant. (If prompted, install the Office Assistant by clicking Yes.)

    b　Right-click the Office Assistant and choose Options to open the Office Assistant dialog box.

    c　Clear Use the Office Assistant and click OK.

7　Dock the Formatting toolbar below the Standard toolbar.

8　If the Getting Started task pane is not displayed, choose View, Task Pane.

9　Close PowerPoint.

10　If necessary, hide the language bar. To do so:

    a　Choose Start, Settings, Control Panel.

    b　Double-click Text Services to open the Text Services dialog box.

    c　Click the Language Bar button under Preferences to open the Language Bar Settings dialog box.

    d　Clear Show the language bar on the desktop.

    e　Click OK.

11　Start Excel. Then, dock the Formatting toolbar below the Standard toolbar. When you're done, close Excel.

12　If necessary, reset any defaults that you have changed. If you don't want to reset the defaults, you can still re-key the course, but some activities might not work exactly as documented.

13 Create a folder called Student Data at the root of the hard drive.
14 If necessary, download the Student Data files for the course. (If you don't have an Internet connection, you can ask your instructor for a copy of the data files on a disk.)
   a Connect to www.courseilt.com/instructor_tools.html.
   b Click the link for Microsoft PowerPoint 2003 to display a page of course listings, and then click the link for PowerPoint 2003: Advanced, Second Edition.
   c Click the link for downloading the Student Data files, and follow the instructions that appear on your screen.
15 Copy the data files to the Student Data folder.

CertBlaster test preparation for Microsoft Office Specialist certification

If you are interested in attaining Microsoft Office Specialist certification, you can download CertBlaster test preparation software for PowerPoint 2003 from the Course ILT Web site. Here's what you do:

1 Go to www.courseilt.com/certblaster.
2 Click the link for PowerPoint 2003.
3 Save the .EXE file to a folder on your hard drive. (**Note**: If you skip this step, the CertBlaster software will not install correctly.)
4 Click Start and choose Run.
5 Click Browse and then navigate to the folder that contains the .EXE file.
6 Select the .EXE file and click Open.
7 Click OK and follow the on-screen instructions. When prompted for the password, enter **c_powerpoint**.

Unit 1
Building custom presentations

Unit time: 60 minutes

Complete this unit, and you'll know how to:

A Modify the designs in an existing template.

B Build a custom template from a blank presentation, and add graphic elements to it.

C Build a custom slide master by using toolbar and menu options.

D Create duplicate slide masters, edit a title master, apply a slide master to selected slides, and rename a slide master.

Topic A: Modifying templates

This topic covers the following Microsoft Office Specialist exam objective.

#	Objective
PP03S-2-6	Customizing templates

Ways to modify templates

Explanation

When you create a PowerPoint presentation, it's based on a template, which includes all the pre-designed formats. The presentation uses the color schemes and design elements of the template, giving the presentation a consistent look. You can modify a template by changing its color scheme, graphics, and fonts in Master view. Any changes you make to the template will be reflected in all the slides in a presentation based on that template.

Do it!

A-1: Modifying a template

Here's how	Here's why
1 Open Microsoft PowerPoint	Choose Start, Programs, Microsoft Office, Microsoft Office PowerPoint 2003.
2 Choose **File, Open...**	To open the Open dialog box.
Navigate to the current unit folder	
Select **Justification**	(If necessary.) You'll modify this template.
Click **Open**	
3 Choose **File, Save As...**	
From the Save as type list, select **Design Template**	(You'll need to scroll down.) To save the presentation as a template. The template will be saved with the .pot file extension in the Templates folder.
Edit the File name box to read **My justification**	
4 Click **Save**	To save the template in the Templates folder.
5 Choose **View, Master, Slide Master**	To switch to Master view.
Observe the Slide Master View toolbar	The Slide Master View toolbar appears when you switch to Master view.
Move the toolbar to one side	To see the entire slide.

6	Select the Master Title Area	You'll change the format of the title.
	Click **B**	(The Bold button is on the Formatting toolbar.) To make the title bold.
	Click **U**	(The Underline button is on the Formatting toolbar.) To underline the title.
7	Double-click as shown	
		(Double-click outside the Master Title Area but on the slide.) To open the Format Object dialog box.
8	Under Fill, from the Color list, select the color as shown	
	Click **OK**	To close the Format Object dialog box.
9	Click **Close Master View**	(The Close Master View button is on the Slide Master View toolbar.) To switch to Normal view.
10	Update and close the template	
11	Open Outlander Spices	(From the current unit folder.) You'll apply the modified template to this presentation.
12	Save the presentation as **My Outlander Spices**	In the current unit folder.
13	Click Design	(The Design button is on the Formatting toolbar.) To open the Slide Design task pane.
14	In the Slide Design task pane, under Available For Use, click the indicated template	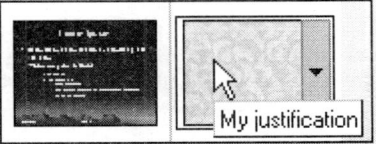
		The template is applied to all the slides in the presentation.
15	Update and close the presentation	

Topic B: Building custom templates

This topic covers the following Microsoft Office Specialist exam objective.

#	Objective
PP03S-2-3	Customizing slide backgrounds

Creating templates from blank presentations

Explanation

PowerPoint provides several built-in templates. However, you can also create your own custom templates. Before you build your own template, you need to decide whether it'll be used to create 35mm slides, overhead transparencies, or a slide show. Accordingly, you can select the template's color scheme, fonts, and graphics.

To create a template, start with a new, blank presentation and customize it. This is the ideal approach because a blank presentation that is based on the default template has minimal formatting associated with it, giving you a clean slate to build on. After you apply the color scheme, styles, and formatting, you save the presentation as a template. Templates are saved with the .pot file extension.

To build a custom template:

1. Choose File, New to display the New Presentation task pane.
2. Under New, click Blank presentation.
3. Select a slide layout.
4. Switch to Master view.
5. Choose Format, Background to open the Background dialog box.
6. Select a background color scheme and a shading style.
7. Click Apply to All to apply formatting to the entire presentation, including the corresponding slide master.
8. Choose File, Save As to open the Save As dialog box.
9. From the Save as type list, select Design Template, and then click Save. PowerPoint will assign the .pot file extension automatically.

Do it!

B-1: Creating a template from a blank presentation

Here's how	Here's why
1 Choose **File, New...**	The New Presentation task pane appears. You'll create a custom template from a blank presentation.
2 Under New, click **Blank presentation**	In the New Presentation task pane.
3 Verify that the Title Slide layout is selected	
4 Switch to Master view	Choose View, Master, Slide Master.

5	Choose **Format, Background...**	(To open the Background dialog box.) You'll apply a custom background to the template.
6	From the Background fill list, select as shown	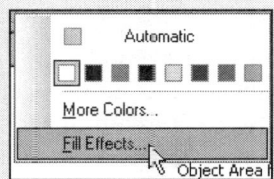
		To open the Fill Effects dialog box.
	Verify that the Gradient tab is activated	
7	Under Colors, select **Two colors**	
	From the Color 1 list, select a green color	You'll apply green as the first color.
	From the Color 2 list, select the white color	You'll apply white as the second color
	Click **OK**	To close the Fill Effects dialog box.
8	Click **Preview**	To preview the color settings on the slide.
9	Click **Apply to All**	To change the background of the entire presentation, including the corresponding slide master.
10	Choose **File, Save As...**	To open the Save As dialog box.
11	From the Save as type list, select **Design Template**	To save the presentation as a template.
	Edit the File name box to read **Spices**	To specify a name for the template.
12	Click **Save**	To save the template in the Templates folder.

Adding graphics to templates

Explanation

Adding graphics to your template helps catch your audiences' attention. Graphic elements can also make a PowerPoint template visually appealing. For example, for business presentations, it's a good idea to have the company logo on every slide. When you add the logo, use either a GIF or a JPEG image if possible because these formats are the standard image formats used on the Web. Using these formats enables you to export your presentation to a Web site.

To insert images into a template, switch to Master view and then choose Insert, Picture, From File.

Do it!

B-2: Adding graphics to a template

Here's how	Here's why
1 Choose **Insert, Picture, From File...**	(To open the Insert Picture dialog box.) You'll insert a picture in the Spices template.
Observe the Files of type list	By default, this dialog box displays a list of all file types for pictures.
2 Navigate to the current unit folder	To display a list of the picture files.
3 Select **Logo**	
4 Click **Insert**	(To insert the graphic into the slide master.) Notice that the Picture toolbar appears.
Observe the graphic	The graphic appears in the center of the slide.

Building custom presentations **1–7**

5	Drag the graphic to the upper-right corner of the slide, as shown	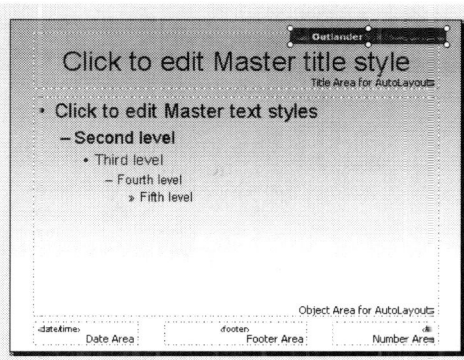
		Use the arrow keys to move the selected object by small increments.
6	Click **Close Master View**	(The Close Master View button is on the Slide Master View toolbar.) To switch to Normal view.
7	Update and close the template	

Topic C: Building custom slide masters

This topic covers the following Microsoft Office Specialist exam objective.

#	Objective
PP03S-2-7	Inserting content in headers and footers (This objective is also covered in *PowerPoint 2003: Basic*, in the unit titled "Modifying presentations.")

Adding symbols to footers

Explanation

Similar to adding a company logo, you can add other symbols to a presentation. For example, you might want to insert the copyright symbol at the bottom of every slide in a presentation. To do so, insert the symbol in the Footer Area of the slide master.

You can create your own symbol or use one of the symbols provided by PowerPoint. To add a built-in symbol, choose Insert, Symbol to open the Symbol dialog box, as shown in Exhibit 1-1. Select a symbol, and click the Insert button. After inserting the symbol, you can resize and format it by selecting it and using the Formatting toolbar.

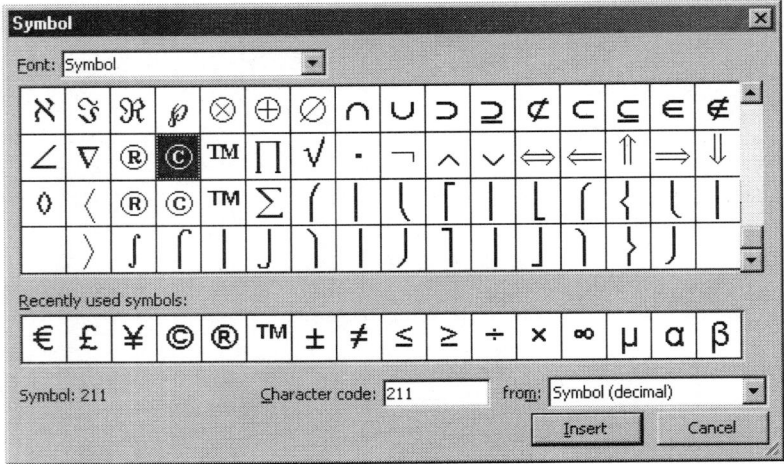

Exhibit 1-1: The Symbol dialog box

Building custom presentations **1–9**

Do it! **C-1: Adding a symbol to the footer**

Here's how	Here's why
1 Open Brand logo	From the current unit folder.
2 Save the presentation as **My brand logo**	
3 Switch to Master view	
4 In the Footer Area, select **<footer>**	You'll insert a copyright symbol into the footer. The text you add to the slide master footer will appear at the bottom of every slide in your presentation.
5 Choose **Insert, Symbol…**	To open the Symbol dialog box.
6 From the Font list, select **Symbol**	The window displays a different set of symbols.
7 Click the copyright symbol as shown	
8 Click **Insert**	To add the copyright symbol to the footer.
9 Click **Close**	To close the Symbol dialog box.
10 Select ©	(In the Footer Area.) You'll change the symbol you just inserted.
Click	To right-align the symbol in the Footer Area.
11 Deselect all placeholders	
12 Update the presentation	

Inserting an object in footers

Explanation

In addition to putting text and symbols in a footer, you can also insert an object in the Footer Area so that the object will appear on every slide. For example, you can switch to Master view and create a WordArt object, and then move it to the Footer Area.

Inserting WordArt

To begin using WordArt, click the Insert WordArt button on the Drawing toolbar. This opens the WordArt Gallery dialog box, shown in Exhibit 1-2.

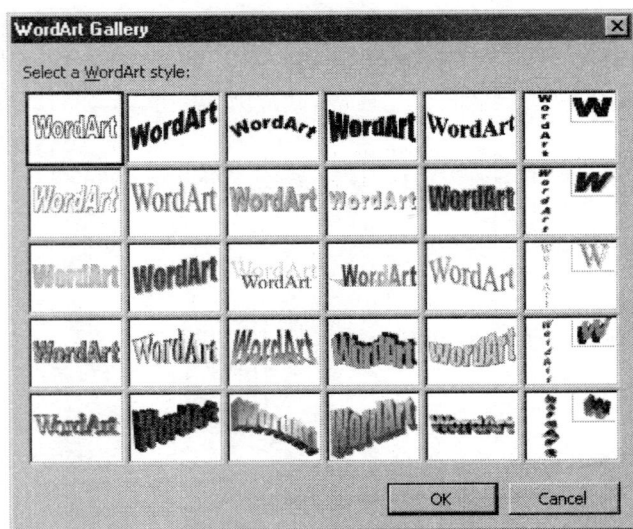

Exhibit 1-2: The WordArt Gallery dialog box

Building custom presentations

Do it!

C-2: Inserting an object in the footer

Here's how	Here's why
1 Click [icon]	(The Insert WordArt button is on the Drawing toolbar.) To open the WordArt Gallery dialog box.
2 Click the indicated WordArt style	
Click **OK**	To open the Edit WordArt Text dialog box.
3 Edit the text to read **Web Expansion 2003**	
Click **OK**	The WordArt logo is inserted in the slide master. The WordArt toolbar also appears.
4 Right-click the WordArt	To view a shortcut menu.
From the shortcut menu, select **Format WordArt...**	To open the Format WordArt dialog box.
Click the **Size** tab	You'll size the WordArt so that it fits in the Footer Area.
Under Scale, check **Lock aspect ratio**	To maintain the proportional height and width of the object when you scale it.
5 Under Scale, in the Height box, enter **50%**	To reduce the size of the WordArt.
Press TAB	
Under Scale, observe the Width box	The value in the Width box has changed to 50% automatically. This occurred because Lock aspect ratio was checked.
Under Size and rotate, observe the Height and Width boxes	The values in these boxes have also changed automatically.
6 Click **OK**	To close the Format WordArt dialog box.
7 Move the logo to the Footer Area as shown	
	To make it a footer object.

8	Click ![paint bucket icon]	(The Format WordArt button is on the WordArt toolbar.) To open the Format WordArt dialog box.
	Click the **Colors and Lines** tab	
	Under Fill, from the Color list, select an orange color	
	Click **OK**	To change the color of the logo to orange.
9	Click 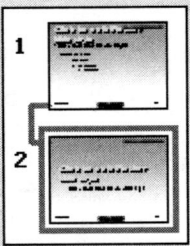	(The Insert New Title Master button is on the Slide Master View toolbar.) To insert a title master.
	Observe the left pane	

The first master is the slide master, and the second master is the title master. Notice that all the formatting you applied to the slide master is automatically copied to the title master.

10	Switch to Normal view	
	Move to the first slide	If necessary.
	Click ![slide show icon]	(To run the presentation.) You'll see that both slides are now formatted according to the changes you made to the slide master.
	Switch to Normal view	
11	Update the presentation	

Topic D: Advanced slide master techniques

Explanation

Once you know how to use slide masters, you can duplicate them, edit them, rename them, and apply them to selected slides.

Duplicating slide masters

By duplicating a slide master, you can save yourself some work. For example, say you want to use a sales presentation for three individual clients, but the presentation needs to have each client's company logo on each slide. Instead of creating three presentations, you can use just one presentation with multiple slide masters. You create duplicate slide masters, with each master containing a client's logo. To customize the presentation, you switch to Normal view and select the slide master you want to apply.

By default, a presentation stores only one set of slide masters. To create a duplicate slide master, switch to Master view, and choose Insert, Duplicate Slide Master.

Do it!

D-1: Duplicating a slide master

Here's how	Here's why
1 Switch to Master view	
2 Choose **Insert, Duplicate Slide Master**	(To create a duplicate set of the slide master.) Move the Slide Master View toolbar, if necessary.
Observe the left pane	Masters three and four are duplicates of masters one and two, respectively. The preserve icon, shaped like a thumbtack, is visible below the numbers 3 and 4 next to the third and fourth masters.
3 Select the first master	

4	Click [icon]	(The Preserve Master button is on the Slide Master View toolbar.) To ensure that both slide masters are preserved with the presentation.
	Observe the fourth master	It has the preserve icon. It's not necessary for all the slides to have the preserve icon. However, at least one master from a slide-title master set should be preserved.
5	Update the presentation	

Editing duplicate slide masters

Explanation

You can edit either the slide master or the title master from a slide-title master set to change the appearance of your presentation. To do this, switch to Master view, select the master that you want to edit, and make your changes in the various placeholders.

Do it!

D-2: Editing a duplicate slide master

Here's how	Here's why
1 Select the fourth master	You'll edit this master.
2 Select the Master title area	(If necessary.) You'll customize the formatting of the title.
3 Click as shown	
From the Font Size list, select **44**	
4 Choose **Format, Font...**	To open the Font dialog box.
5 From the Color list, select an orange color	From the Color list, select More Colors and then select the color.
Click **OK**	To close the Colors dialog box.
Click **OK**	To close the Font dialog box.
Hold (SHIFT) and click the third master	(To select the set.) You'll change the background for this set of masters.
Release (SHIFT)	

Building custom presentations   1–15

6	Choose **Format, Background...**	To open the Background dialog box.
7	From the Background fill list, select as shown	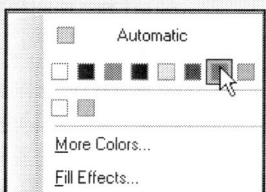

You'll apply this color to the background.

8	Click **Apply**	
	Switch to Normal view	
9	Click **Design**	(The Slide Design button is on the Formatting toolbar.) To display the Slide Design task pane.
	Under Used in This Presentation, observe the two design templates	These are the two slide masters.
10	Click as shown	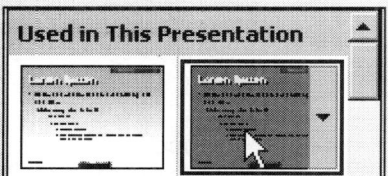

The new master is applied to the presentation. Notice that all the slides have been updated.

11	Click as shown	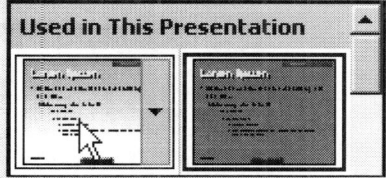

To revert to the old master.

12 Update the presentation

Applying slide masters to selected slides

Explanation

To apply a slide master to only selected slides:

1. Select the slides to which you want to apply the slide master.
2. In the Slide Design task pane, from the Used in This Presentation list, click the arrow to the right of the template to display several options.
3. From the options, select Apply to Selected Slides.

Do it!

D-3: Applying a slide master to selected slides

Here's how	Here's why
1 Click ⊞	To switch to Slide Sorter view.
2 Select the second slide	You'll apply the duplicate slide master settings to this slide.
3 Click as shown	To display the slide options.
4 Choose **Apply to Selected Slides**	To apply this master to the second slide.
Observe the two slides	The two slides have different slide masters applied to them.
5 Update the presentation	

Building custom presentations **1–17**

Renaming slide masters

Explanation If you're using different slide masters in a presentation, you can differentiate between these masters by renaming them. You rename slide masters by using the Rename Master button on the Slide Master View toolbar.

To rename a slide master:
1. Click the Rename Master button on the Slide Master View toolbar to open the Rename Master dialog box.
2. Type a name for the slide master.
3. Click Rename to close the dialog box.

Do it! **D-4: Renaming a slide master**

Here's how	Here's why
1 Switch to Master view	
2 Move the mouse pointer over the fourth master as shown	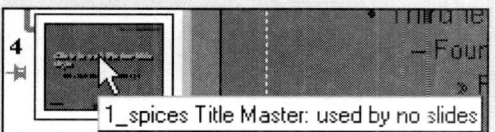
	A ScreenTip appears, showing the name of the master and the number of slides to which this master is applied.
3 Select the fourth master	You'll rename this slide master.
4 Click ![button]	(The Rename Master button is on the Slide Master View toolbar.) The Rename Master dialog box appears.
5 Edit the Master name box to read **My master**	
Click **Rename**	To rename the slide master and close the dialog box.
6 Point to the fourth master	
	A ScreenTip appears, stating the name of the slide master and the number of slides to which this master is applied.
7 Update and close the presentation	

Unit summary: Building custom presentations

Topic A In this topic, you learned how to **modify** a template in **Master view**.

Topic B In this topic, you learned how to create a **custom template** from a blank presentation. You specified a **template color scheme** by using the Background dialog box. You also **added graphic elements** to a template by using the Insert menu.

Topic C In this topic, you learned how to build a **custom slide master**. You learned how to add a **symbol** and a **WordArt object** at the bottom of every slide in a presentation by inserting them in the Footer Area of the slide master.

Topic D In this topic, you learned how to **duplicate slide masters**, **edit** a title master, **apply a master to selected slides**, and **rename** a slide master.

Independent practice activity

1. Open Spices.
2. Save the template as **Practice template**. (*Hint:* In the Save As dialog box, from the Save as type list, select Design Template.)
3. Switch to Master view.
4. Modify the background color scheme by using a Fill Effect with a two-color gradient.
5. Update and close the template.
6. Create a new presentation based on the template created in Step 5. (*Hint*: In the New Presentation task pane, under Templates, choose On my computer.)
7. Change the Shading style that's applied to the background. (*Hint:* Use the Fill Effects dialog box.)
8. Change the font size, and apply bold formatting to the text in the Master Title Area.
9. Create a duplicate master. Preserve all the masters.
10. On the duplicate master, change the background color, and format the text differently from the way you did in Step 9.
11. Create a WordArt logo for the **Expansion 2003** project.
12. Add the logo to the Footer Area.
13. Switch to Normal view. Add a new slide to the presentation, and apply the new master to this slide.
14. Save the presentation as **My practice logo** in the current unit folder. Close the presentation.

Review questions

1 Any changes you make to a template will be reflected in all the slides in a presentation based on that template. True or False?

2 Templates are saved with what file extension?

3 If you want to export a presentation to the Web, and this presentation contains graphics, it's a good idea to use standard image formats. List two standard image formats used on the Web.

4 List the steps used to add a built-in symbol to a footer.

5 List the steps used to rename a slide master.

Unit 2
Using multimedia in presentations

Unit time: 70 minutes

Complete this unit, and you'll know how to:

A Use advanced clip art and drawing techniques.

B Add sound and movie clips to a presentation.

C Add animation effects to a presentation.

D Add scanned images to a presentation.

Topic A: Advanced clip art and drawing techniques

This topic covers the following Microsoft Office Specialist exam objectives.

#	Objective
PP03S-2-2	Adding effects to pictures, shapes and other graphics (This objective is also covered in *PowerPoint 2003: Basic*, in the unit titled "Working with graphics.")
PP03S-2-2	Aligning, connecting and rotating pictures, shapes and other graphics (This objective is also covered in *PowerPoint 2003: Basic*, in the unit titled "Using drawing tools.")

Clip art and the Picture toolbar

Explanation

The term *clip art* refers to pre-designed pictures, animations, sounds, and movies that you can insert into PowerPoint slides to give a presentation more impact. PowerPoint 2003 provides several clip art objects. After you insert a clip art object, you can crop, recolor, resize, rotate, or scale the object as needed by using the Picture toolbar, shown in Exhibit 2-1. You can display the Picture toolbar by choosing View, Toolbars, Picture, or by selecting any picture on a slide.

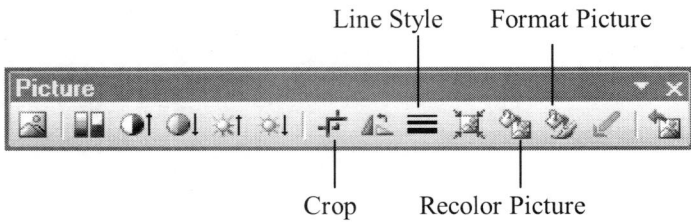

Exhibit 2-1: The Picture toolbar

Cropping clip art

When you add a clip art object to a presentation, the object retains its default design settings, including size, color, and scaling. To add only a portion of a clip art object to a slide, you need to insert the full image and then crop it. If necessary, you can restore it to its original settings later.

To crop a clip art object:

1. Select the clip art object.
2. Click the Crop button on the Picture toolbar.
3. Point to a sizing handle. The pointer changes to a cropping tool.
4. Drag the sizing handle to crop the object.
5. Deselect the object.

Using multimedia in presentations 2–3

Do it!

A-1: Cropping a clip art object

Here's how	Here's why
1 Open Training	(From the current unit folder.) You'll crop the clip art object on the first slide in this presentation.
2 Save the presentation as **My training**	In the current unit folder.
3 Verify that the first slide is selected	Move to the first slide, if necessary.
4 Select the clip art	
	You'll crop the object so that the airplane is not visible.
Observe the Picture toolbar	This toolbar appears automatically when you select any picture object.
5 Click	(The Crop button is on the Picture toolbar.) To activate the cropping tool.
Observe the pointer	
	It changes to a cropping tool.
6 Point to the upper-center sizing handle	

7 Drag the sizing handle as shown	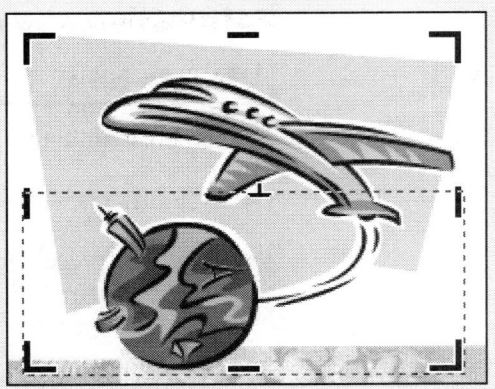	
	To crop the upper portion of the picture.	
Crop and reposition the object as shown		
	Use the sizing handle to crop the object. Then drag the object to reposition it.	
Deselect the cropping tool	Click anywhere away from the object, or click the Crop button again.	
8 Update the presentation		

Formatting clip art

Explanation

You can customize a clip art object by changing its color, adding a background color, or modifying its line style. To recolor an object, you use the Recolor Picture dialog box. Use the Format Picture dialog box to add a background color or modify line styles.

Using the Recolor Picture dialog box

By default, all clip art objects have predefined color schemes. However, these color settings can be customized. To recolor an object:

1. Select the clip art object.
2. Click the Recolor Picture button on the Picture toolbar to open the Recolor Picture dialog box.
3. Under New, use the drop-down lists to change the colors. The right side of the dialog box displays a preview of the object with the new color settings.
4. Click the Preview button to view the recolored object on the slide.
5. If the new colors are acceptable, click OK to close the Recolor Picture dialog box.
6. Deselect the clip art object.

Using the Format Picture dialog box

You can also add a background fill and lines to a clip art object. To add a background fill, click the Format Picture button on the Picture toolbar. This opens the Format Picture dialog box; then click the Colors and Lines tab, shown in Exhibit 2-2. Under Fill, use the Color list to select a fill color. You can add a line to the clip art object by using the various options under Line.

You can also add line styles to a clip art object by selecting the object and clicking the Line Style button on the Picture toolbar.

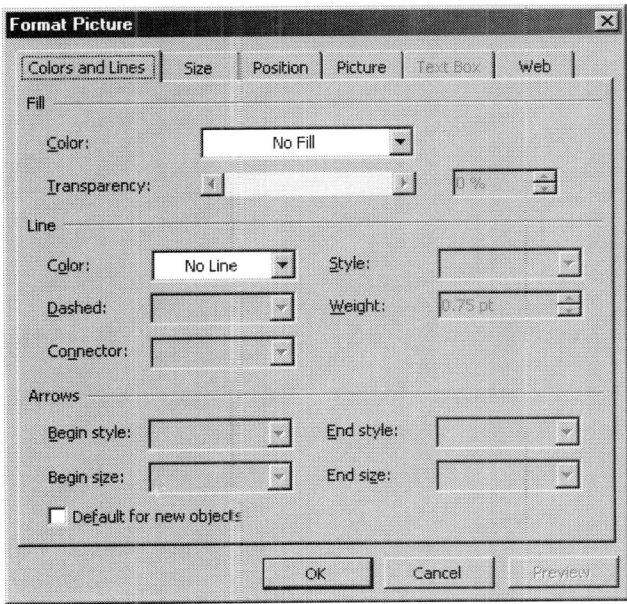

Exhibit 2-2: The Colors and Lines tab of the Format Picture dialog box

A-2: Modifying clip art colors, background fills, and lines

Here's how	Here's why
1 Move to the sixth slide	You'll recolor the clip art on this slide.
2 Select the clip art object	
3 Click [button]	(The Recolor Picture button is on the Picture toolbar.) To open the Recolor Picture dialog box. This dialog box shows the clip art and a list of all the colors used in it. You can change any color and preview the results before applying the new color.
4 Under New, display the last drop-down list as shown	
	To view the available colors.
Select the color as shown	
Click **Preview**	A preview of the clip art with its new color settings appears on the slide. You might need to move the dialog box to see the clip art on the slide.
5 Click **OK**	To apply the new color and to close the Recolor Picture dialog box.
6 Move to the second slide	You'll add a background fill to the clip art on this slide.
Select the clip art	

Using multimedia in presentations **2–7**

7	Click [icon]	(The Format Picture button is on the Picture toolbar.) To open the Format Picture dialog box.
	Click the **Colors and Lines** tab	
	Under Fill, from the Color list, select the tan color	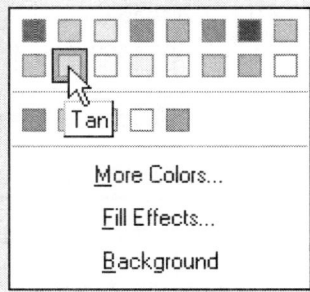
		To apply a tan background to the clip art object.
	Under Line, from the Color list, select **Automatic**	To apply the default line settings.
	Click **OK**	To apply the settings and to close the Format Picture dialog box.
8	Move to the fifth slide	You'll add lines to the clip art on this side.
9	Select the clip art object	
10	Click [icon]	(The Line Style button is on the Picture toolbar.) To display a list of available line styles
	From the list, select **6 pt**	To add a 6-point black border around the clip art.
	Deselect the clip art	Notice the new line around the clip art.
11	Update the presentation	

Rotating objects

Explanation

You can rotate an object either clockwise or counterclockwise to change its orientation on a slide. You can also flip an object horizontally or vertically.

To rotate an object, click the Draw button on the Drawing toolbar, choose Rotate or Flip, and then choose an option from the submenu. To rotate an object to any angle, you can use the Free Rotate tool on the Drawing toolbar.

Do it!

A-3: Rotating an object

Here's how	Here's why
1 Move to the second slide	
2 Select **Marketing**	You'll rotate the title text on this slide.
3 Click **Draw**	The Draw button is on the Drawing toolbar.
Select as shown	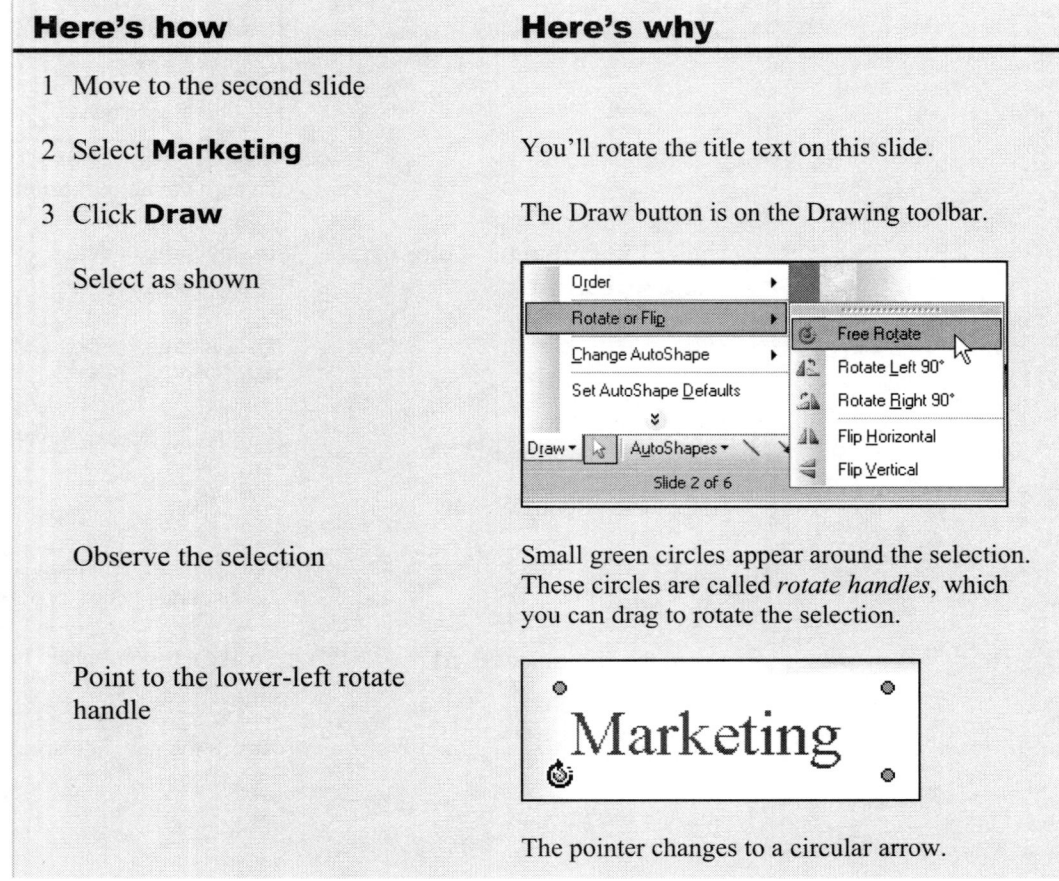
Observe the selection	Small green circles appear around the selection. These circles are called *rotate handles*, which you can drag to rotate the selection.
Point to the lower-left rotate handle	
	The pointer changes to a circular arrow.

Using multimedia in presentations 2-9

4 Rotate the text as shown	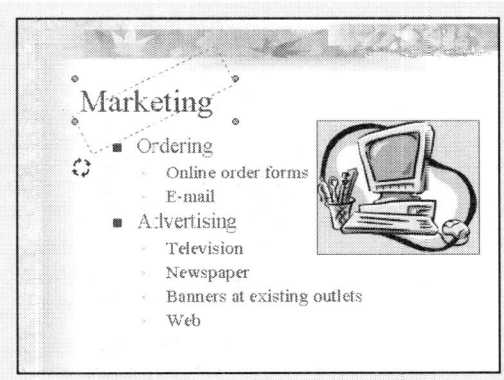
5 Click outside the selection	To deactivate the rotation tool.
6 Move to the sixth slide	You'll rotate the clip art in this slide.
7 Select the clip art	
8 Click **Draw**	The Draw button is on the Drawing toolbar. A menu appears.
Choose **Rotate or Flip**, **Free Rotate**	
Point to the lower-left rotate handle	
9 Rotate the clip art as shown	
10 Deactivate the rotation tool	Click anywhere outside the clip art.
11 Update the presentation	

Topic B: Adding movies and sound

This topic covers the following Microsoft Office Specialist exam objective.

#	Objective
PP03S-1-5	Inserting objects (e.g., Excel charts, media clips, Paintbrush pictures) (This objective is also covered in *PowerPoint 2003: Basic*, in the units titled "Working with graphics" and "Using tables and charts.")

Adding movie clips

Explanation

You can add a movie clip from a file or from the Clip Organizer. PowerPoint's built-in movie clips, also called *motion clips*, are organized into various collections. To select a clip from one of these collections, choose Insert, Movies and Sounds, Movie from Clip Organizer. This step lists all the clips in the task pane. The clips are listed in the form of thumbnail images. You can change the search options by clicking the Modify button in the task pane and changing the search and media criteria. You can then add a clip by clicking it.

Do it!

B-1: Adding a movie clip

Here's how	Here's why
1 Move to the fourth slide	You'll add a movie clip to this slide.
2 Choose **Insert**, **Movies and Sounds**, **Movie from File…**	To open the Insert Movie dialog box.
3 Navigate to the current unit folder	
4 Select **Outlander movie**	If necessary.
Click **OK**	A message box appears, asking you how to start the movie in the slide show.
Click **Automatically**	To specify that the movie should play automatically during the slide show. The first picture of the movie clip appears on the slide.
5 Position the clip as shown	
Deselect the clip	

Using multimedia in presentations 2-11

6 Click 🖳	To start the slide show. You'll see that the movie clip plays on the slide.
7 Switch to Normal view	
8 Update the presentation	

Adding sound clips

Explanation

You can increase the impact of a presentation by adding sound clips to it. PowerPoint's built-in sound clips are organized into various collections. To select a clip from one of these collections, choose Insert, Movies and Sounds, Sound from Clip Organizer to list all the clips in the task pane. You can then select and insert a sound clip of your choice.

When you add sound to a slide, a sound icon appears on the slide. Then, a message box prompts you to specify whether you want the sound to play automatically or only when you click the sound icon.

Do it!

B-2: Adding a sound clip

Here's how	Here's why
1 Move to the sixth slide	If necessary.
2 Choose **Insert**, **Movies and Sounds**, **Sound from File...**	To open the Insert Sound dialog box.
3 Navigate to the current unit folder	
4 Select **APPLAUSE**	(If necessary.) You'll insert this sound clip.
Click **OK**	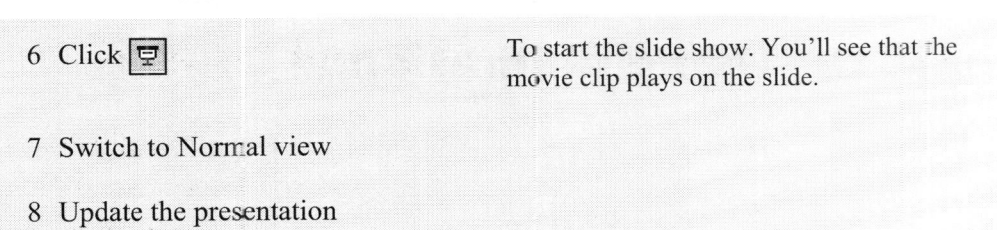
	A message box appears, asking you how to start the sound clip in the slide show.
Click **Automatically**	To specify that the sound clip should play automatically during the slide show. Notice that a sound icon appears on the slide.
5 Move the sound icon to the lower-left corner of the slide	
6 Switch to Slide Show view	The sound you selected plays automatically.
Switch to Normal view	
7 Update the presentation	

Topic C: Using animations

This topic covers the following Microsoft Office Specialist exam objective.

#	Objective
PP03S-2-4	Applying an animation scheme to a single slide, group of slides, or an entire presentation

Animating objects

Explanation

In PowerPoint, an animation effect provides the illusion of movement on a slide. For example, you can have bullet items displayed one at a time or make them "fly in" from any side of the slide.

To animate an object, you use the Custom Animation task pane. This helps you add entry or exit animations, control timing, and synchronize all the effects. You can add animation effects to a single object or multiple objects. For example, you can animate bullet text to appear one letter at a time, one word at a time, or one paragraph at a time. When you animate an object, it's indicated on the slide by an animation tag, as shown in Exhibit 2-3. These tags are non-printing, and they are visible on screen only in Normal view with the Custom Animation task pane open.

You can specify the order and timing of animations. For example, you can set them to occur automatically or only after you click the mouse. You can also preview the animation text and other objects to see how the animation slide plays.

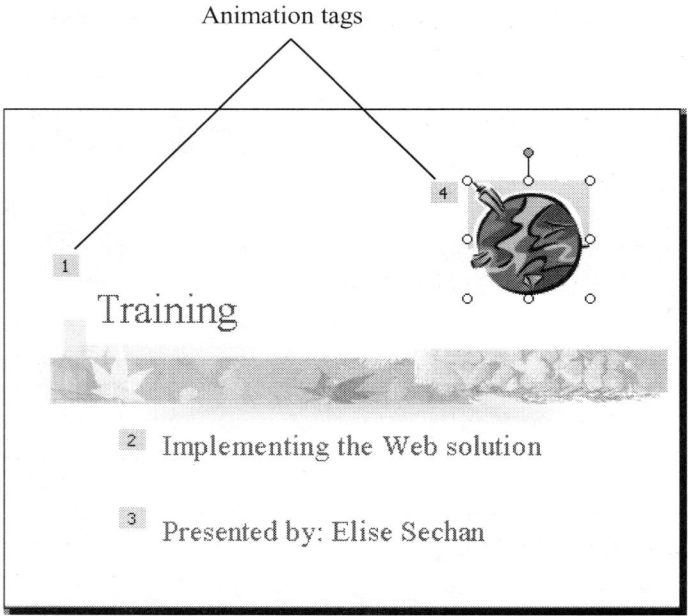

Exhibit 2-3: A sample slide with animation tags

Do it!   **C-1: Animating an object**

Here's how	Here's why
1 Move to the first slide	
2 Choose **Slide Show, Custom Animation...**	To display the Custom Animation task pane. Notice that AutoPreview is checked by default.
3 Select **Training**	You'll apply an animation effect to the title.
4 From the Custom Animation task pane, click **Add Effect**	
Select as shown	
	The title Training flies in from the bottom of the slide. Notice that an animation tag appears next to the title.
5 In the Custom Animation task pane, observe the Start list	The animation will run on clicking.
6 In the Custom Animation task pane, from the Direction list, select **From Right**	The title flies into the slide from the right side.
7 In the Custom Animation task pane, from the Speed list, select **Fast**	To adjust the speed at which the title appears.
8 Select the subtitle placeholder	
9 Apply the Fly In effect to the selected placeholder	(Click Add Effect, and select Fly In from the Entrance list.) The two lines fly in one by one from the bottom of the slide.
Change the direction to **From Right**	Use the Direction list.

10 Select the clip art

11 From the Custom Animation task pane, click **Add Effect** and select as shown

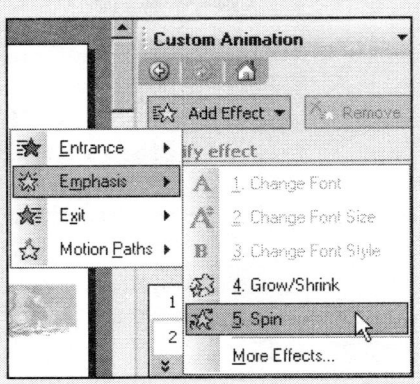

The globe will now have the spin effect.

12 In the Custom Animation task pane, click **Play** (Located near the bottom of the pane.) To play the animation effects you have added.

13 Update the presentation

Organizing animation effects

Explanation

After applying various animation effects to a slide, you can reorder them to change the sequence. A slide consists of a title, a bulleted list, and graphics. To make your presentation visually appealing, you might want to order the elements so that the graphic appears first, followed by the title and the bulleted list. For example, while running business presentations, you might want to display the company's logo first, followed by the title and then text.

To reorder the effects, select an effect from the list of effects in the Custom Animation task pane, and click the Up or Down Re-Order buttons.

Using multimedia in presentations **2–15**

Do it! **C-2: Reordering the effects in a slide**

Here's how	Here's why
1 Verify that the first slide is selected	
2 Click as shown 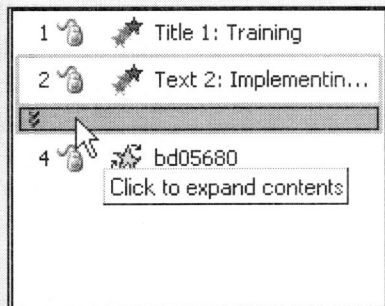	To view all the items in the animation sequence list.
3 Select the fourth effect	(If necessary.) This is the spin effect applied to the clip art.
4 Click the Up Re-Order button as shown 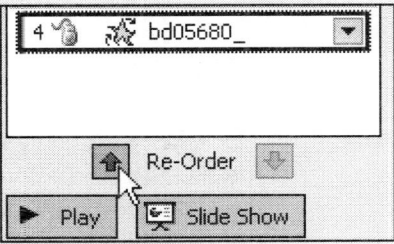	This effect now becomes the third effect in sequence. The effect number changes to 3.
Click the Up Re-Order button twice	To make the selected effect the first effect in the animation sequence.
5 Click **Play**	(In the Custom Animation task pane.) To see the new order of the animation effects.
6 Update the presentation	

Animating slides

Explanation

You can animate a presentation by applying the default animation schemes. You can apply animation schemes to a single slide or to multiple slides. To apply a default animation scheme, choose Slide Show, Animation Schemes to display the Slide Design task pane with the Animation Schemes list. From the list, select an animation scheme.

Do it!

C-3: Applying animation schemes to a presentation

Here's how	Here's why
1 Choose **Slide Show, Animation Schemes…**	The Slide Design task pane appears with the Animation Schemes list.
2 From the Apply to selected slides list, under Exciting, select **Float**	The preview of the slide appears with applied effects.
3 Click **Apply to All Slides**	To apply this animation scheme to the entire presentation. The preview of the slide with applied effects appears.
4 Click **Play**	(In the Custom Animation task pane.) To view the animation effect you have applied to all slides.
Switch to Normal view	
5 Click the sixth slide	To select the slide.
From the Apply to selected slides list, under Subtle, select **Flash bulb**	A preview of the slide appears with the applied effects.
Choose **Slide Show, View Show**	The entire presentation appears with the animation effect you selected. Notice that the animation scheme for the sixth slide is different from the rest of the slides.
Switch to Normal view	
6 Click the third slide	To select the slide.
Hold `CTRL` and click the fourth and fifth slides	To select the fourth and fifth slides.
From the Apply to selected slides list, under Exciting, select **Neutron**	A preview of the slide appears with the applied effects.
Choose **Slide Show, View Show**	The entire presentation appears with the animation effect you selected.
7 Update the presentation	

Topic D: Using scanned images

Explanation

You might want to add photographs to a presentation to show featured products, key personnel, company offices, and so on. You can add pictures in several formats, including bitmap, TIFF, JPEG, and GIF.

Using scanned images

Adding scanned images of photographs is a great way to add life to your presentations. However, the images must be saved in a file format that PowerPoint can accept.

To add a scanned image to a presentation, choose Insert, Picture, From File to open the Insert Picture dialog box. Select an image, and click the Insert button. You can then resize and position the image as needed.

Do it!

D-1: Adding a scanned image to a slide

Here's how	Here's why
1 Move to the last slide	You'll add a new slide at the end of the presentation.
2 Insert a new slide	Click New Slide on the Formatting toolbar.
From the Slide Layout task pane, select the Title Only layout	To apply the selected layout to the new slide.
3 Type **Our team**	In the title area.
4 Choose **Insert, Picture, From File...**	To open the Insert Picture dialog box.
Navigate to the current unit folder	In the Student Data folder.
5 Select **Team**	This scanned image was saved in JPEG format.
Click **Insert**	To add the image to the new slide.
6 Resize and position the image	To improve the slide's appearance.
7 Run the presentation	
8 Update and close the presentation	

Unit summary: Using multimedia in presentations

Topic A In this topic, you learned how to **crop** and **recolor** clip art objects. You **added background fills** and **lines** to clip art objects by using the **Picture toolbar**. You also learned how to **rotate** an object.

Topic B In this topic, you learned about the **Clip Organizer**, and you learned how to **add movie and sound clips** to a presentation.

Topic C In this topic, you learned how to **add animation effects** to text and objects by using the **Animation Effects toolbar**.

Topic D In this topic, you learned how to **add scanned images** to a presentation.

Independent practice activity

1. Open Annual meeting.
2. Save the presentation as **My annual meeting**.
3. Select the clip art object on the first slide.
4. Crop the object to show only three people.
5. Add a white background fill to the object.
6. Apply the 2¼-point line style to the object.
7. Select the clip art object on the second slide.
8. Recolor the object. Preview the new colors on the slide before applying them.
9. Add the Spices movie clip to the slide, and place it in the location of your choice. (The clip is in the current unit folder.)
10. Add a DRUMROLL sound clip (from the current unit folder) to the slide
11. Apply the animation effects of your choice to the clip art object and to the text on each slide.
12. Run the presentation.
13. Update and close the presentation.

Review questions

1 What is clip art?

2 List some ways you can customize a clip art object.

3 What tool is used to rotate an object to any angle?

4 What are motion clips?

5 List the steps used to select a sound clip from one of PowerPoint's built-in sound collections.

6 List the steps used to apply a default animation scheme to a presentation.

Unit 3
Using organization charts and tables

Unit time: 30 minutes

Complete this unit, and you'll know how to:

A Format organization charts.

B Draw and format tables.

Topic A: Advanced organization chart options

Explanation

You can use PowerPoint's organization chart feature to insert a diagram of your company's hierarchy into a presentation. By using the advanced options of the organization chart feature, you can add a new chart design, reformat text, add a border style, or change the background fill color of a chart.

Applying layout styles

You use the Title and Diagram or Organization Chart layout to add a new organization chart to your presentation. Double-click the icon on the layout to open the Diagram Gallery dialog box. Select the Organization Chart diagram, and click OK. A chart template containing four boxes connected by lines, shown in Exhibit 3-1, appears on the slide.

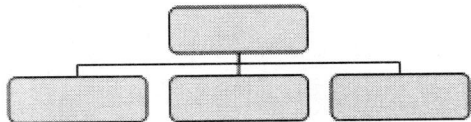

Exhibit 3-1: The default organization chart layout

After you create an organization chart, you can change the arrangement of the boxes by applying a different style.

To apply a new style to an organization chart:

1. Select the organization chart to open the Organization Chart toolbar.
2. Select the first-level box.
3. From the Layout list on the toolbar, select a style.
4. Deselect the chart.

Using organization charts and tables

A-1: Applying a layout style

Do it!

Here's how	Here's why
1 Open Performance	(From the current unit folder.) You'll rearrange the boxes in the organization chart by applying a new style.
2 Save the presentation as **My performance**	
3 Select the organization chart	(The Organization Chart toolbar appears.) You'll edit the chart.
4 Select the first-level box	To change the layout of the second level, you must select the first-level box.
5 Click **Layout** and select as shown	Standard / Both Hanging / Left Hanging / Right Hanging / AutoLayout

The Layout button is on the Organization Chart toolbar. |
6 Click **Fit Text**	On the Organization Chart toolbar. You'll increase the text size on all slides.
7 Resize the chart as shown	Use the resize handles.
8 Update the presentation	

Formatting text

Explanation

You can format text in an organization chart by changing the alignment, font, and color of the text.

To format the text in an organization chart:
1. Select the organization chart to make the Organization Chart toolbar available.
2. Select the text that you want to format.
3. Choose Format, Font to open the Font dialog box.
4. Change the font, size, style, and/or color.
5. Deselect the text.

Do it!

A-2: Formatting text in an organization chart

Here's how	Here's why
1 Select the first-level box	You'll change the font of the text in this box.
2 From the Font list, select **Arial Black**	On the Formatting toolbar.
Change the font size to **16**	
3 Select the first box on the second level	
On the Organization Chart toolbar, click **Select**	
Choose **Level**	The entire second level is now selected.
4 Click ![icon]	(The Align Left button is on the Formatting toolbar.) To left-align the selected text.
5 Change the font size to **16**	
Deselect the selection	
6 Select **Ann Salinski**	You'll change the appearance of this name.

7 From the Font list, select **Arial Black**

   Click I

   Deselect the text

   On the Formatting toolbar.

   The Italic button is on the Formatting toolbar.

8 Apply the same formatting to the names Jack Thomas, Elise Sechan, and Susan Gianni

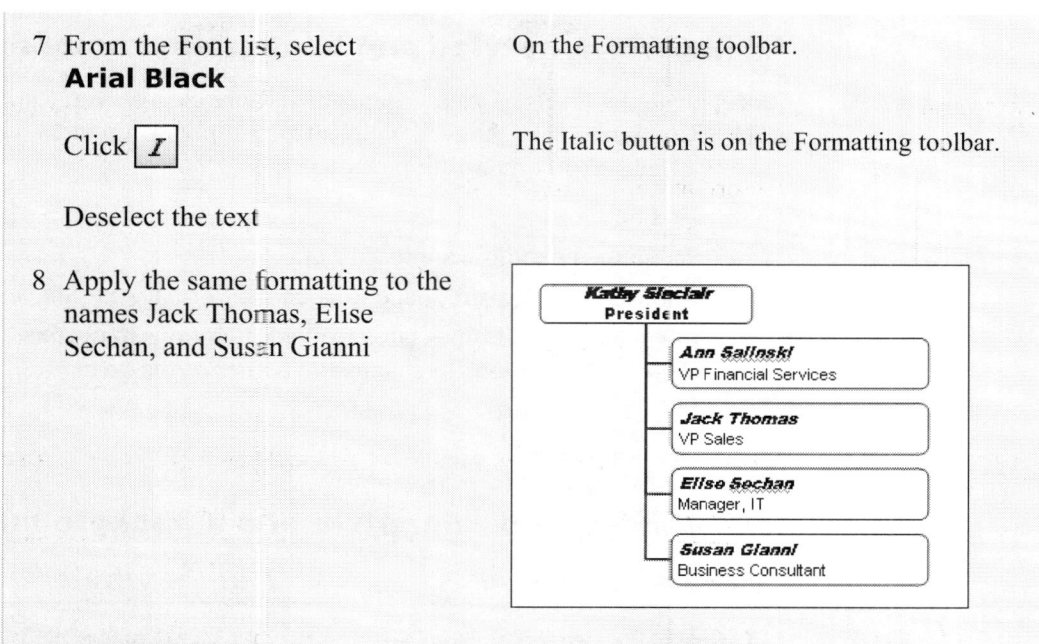

9 Update the presentation

Adding border styles and background colors

Explanation

To delineate the levels of your organization more clearly, you can apply different border styles to the boxes at each level. You can also apply different background colors and shadow effects to an organization chart.

To format a box:
1. Select the box you want to format.
2. Choose Format, AutoShape to open the Format AutoShape dialog box.
3. In the Colors and Lines tab, change Fill options to change the background, and change Line options to change the border of the box.
4. Click OK to close the dialog box.
5. Deselect the box.

Do it!

A-3: Adding a border style and a background color

Here's how	Here's why
1 Select the first-level box	You'll change the background color of this box.
2 Right-click and choose **Format AutoShape...**	To open the Format AutoShape dialog box.
Click the **Colors and Lines** tab	If necessary.
Under Fill, from the Color list, select as shown	To change the color of the box.
3 Under Line, from the Color list, select as shown	To change the color of the border of the box.
4 Click **OK**	To apply the new settings to the box and to close the Format AutoShape dialog box.

Using organization charts and tables 3–7

5	Click ▣	(The Shadow Style button is on the Drawing toolbar.) A menu appears.
6	Click as shown	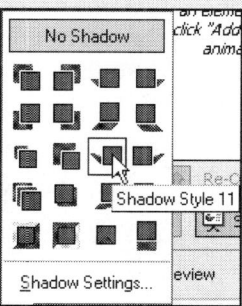 To apply Shadow Style 11 to the AutoShape.
	Observe the first-level box	A shadow appears for the first-level box.
7	Update the presentation	

Organization chart styles

Explanation

PowerPoint has default organization chart styles that you can apply to your charts. To apply a style to a chart, you need to click the Autoformat button on the Organization Chart toolbar. This opens the Organization Chart Style Gallery dialog box. The left side lists all the styles available, and the right side shows a sample of the style, as shown in Exhibit 3-2.

To apply a style:

1 Select the organization chart.
2 Click Autoformat on the Organization Chart toolbar.
3 From the Organization Chart Style Gallery dialog box, select a style.
4 Click Apply to apply the style to your chart.

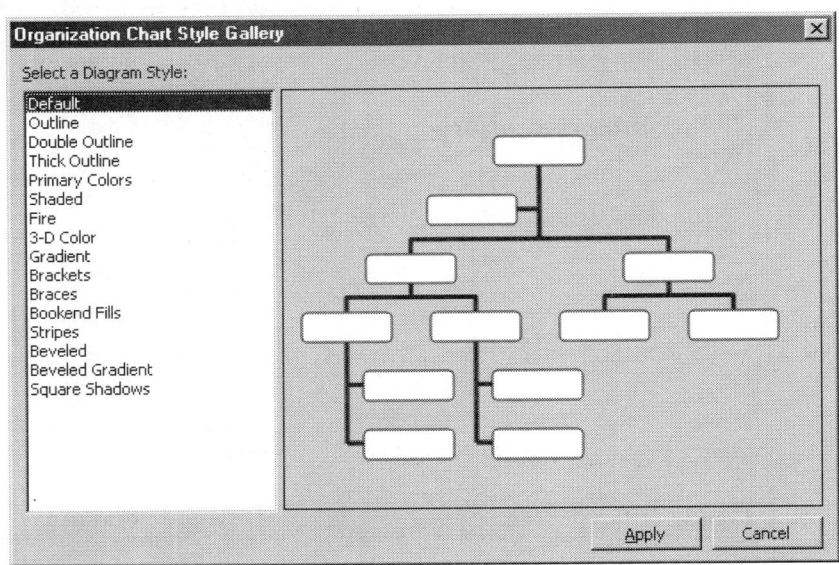

Exhibit 3-2: The Organization Chart Style Gallery dialog box

Do it!

A-4: Applying an organization chart style

Here's how	Here's why
1 Select the chart	If necessary.
2 Click	(The Autoformat button is on the Organization Chart toolbar.) To open the Organization Chart Style Gallery dialog box.
From the list, select **Beveled Gradient**	To apply this style to the box.
Click **OK**	All the boxes now have a beveled shape with a gradient color fill.
3 Update the presentation	

Topic B: Formatting and modifying tables

Explanation

Tables display information in rows and columns. While drawing a table, you can specify the number of rows and columns. You can format a table and align the text in it.

Formatting tables

You can format a table by using the Tables and Borders toolbar, shown in Exhibit 3-3. Using this toolbar, you can change the style, width, and color of the table border. You can use the Fill Color button to change the table's background color.

In addition, you can change the border style and color by using the Format Table dialog box. To open the Format Table dialog box, choose Format, Table. In this dialog box, you can preview the selected border style and color before applying them to the table.

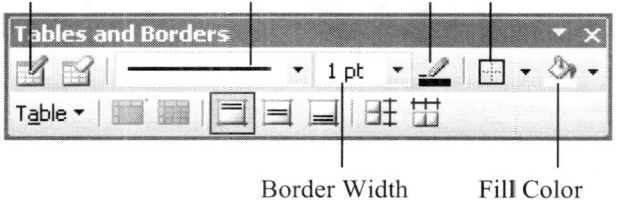

Exhibit 3-3: The Tables and Borders toolbar

Do it!

B-1: Formatting a table

Here's how	Here's why
1 Move to the second slide	
2 Select the table by clicking the border of the table	The Tables and Borders toolbar appears.
3 From the Fill Color list, select **More Fill Colors...**	(Located on the Tables and Borders toolbar.) To open the Colors dialog box.
4 Select the color as shown	
Click **OK**	The fill color of the table changes.

5	Click [icon] Choose **More Border Colors...**	The Border Color button is on the Tables and Borders toolbar. To open the Colors dialog box.
6	Select the color as shown	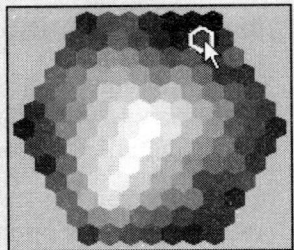
	Click **OK**	
7	From the Border Width list, select **3 pt**	(The Border Width list is on the Tables and Borders toolbar.) To increase the thickness of the border.
8	Click [icon]	(The Outside Borders button is on the Tables and Borders toolbar.) To apply outside borders to the table.
	Deselect the table	
9	Update the presentation	

Formatting text in tables

Explanation

After adding text to a table, you can change the font as well as its size and style. To do this, select the text and open the Font dialog box by choosing Format, Font. Then, make the desired changes, and click OK.

You can use the Format Painter to apply the same settings to other text in your presentation. You can also align the text in a table by using the Formatting toolbar.

Do it!

B-2: Formatting text in a table

Here's how	Here's why
1 Select all of the text in the left column	You'll re-align the text in this column by using the Formatting toolbar.
2 Click ≡	(The Center button is on the Formatting toolbar.) To center the selected text.
3 Select all of the text in the right column	
4 Click ≡	(The Align Left button is on the Formatting toolbar.) To left-align the selected text.
Deselect the text	
Observe the table	The left-column text is centered, and the right-column text is left-aligned.
5 Select **Performance**	You'll change the font.
6 From the Font list, select **Arial Black**	Scroll up, if necessary.
7 Select **Price**	
8 Choose **Format, Font...**	To open the Font dialog box. You'll change the formatting of the selected text.
From the Font list, select **Verdana**	Scroll down, if necessary.
Under Effects, check **Shadow**	
From the Color list, select a blue color	
9 Click **OK**	To close the Font dialog box and apply the new settings.
10 Apply the same formatting to Inventory turnover, Cost, and Profit	
11 Update the presentation	

Drawing tables

Explanation

You can draw a table by using the Tables and Borders toolbar. To display this toolbar, choose View, Toolbars, Tables and Borders. When you use the Draw Table tool, you draw the table border first, followed by the rows and columns in any order. As you draw the table, you can vary the row and column dimensions. You can also use the toolbar to change the border width, color, and style of the table.

After you finish drawing a table, you might want to change the size of the rows or columns. To increase the width of a column, first place the pointer over the line marking the right side of the column. The pointer will change to a double-headed arrow with two vertical lines in between. Then you can then drag to resize the column. You can resize rows in a similar manner. In addition, you can double-click to automatically resize a column to fit the text.

To draw a table by using the Tables and Borders toolbar:

1. Choose View, Toolbars, Tables and Borders.
2. Click the Draw Table button. When you move the pointer over the slide, the pointer changes to a pencil.
3. Click the Border Width drop-down arrow, and select a border width.
4. Click the Border Color button, and select a border color.
5. On the slide, drag to create a table border.
6. Within the table border, drag vertically to create columns, and drag horizontally to create rows.

Do it!

B-3: Drawing a table

Here's how	Here's why
1 Add a new slide	
2 Select the Title Only layout	
3 Change the slide title to **Sales target** Center the title	As the title of the slide.
4 Choose **View, Toolbars, Tables and Borders**	To display the Tables and Borders toolbar.
5 Click	The Draw Table button is on the Tables and Borders toolbar.
Point to the slide	The pointer changes to a pencil that you can drag to create a table border, but do not do this now. You'll first specify a border width and color.

Using organization charts and tables **3–13**

6 Click ✎   (The Border Color button is on the Tables and Borders toolbar.) You'll specify a border color for the table. This color setting will be applied to all of the gridlines in the table.

Choose **More Border Colors...**

Select the color as shown

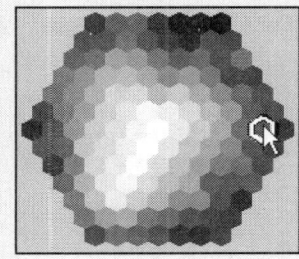

Click **OK**

7 On the slide, drag to draw the table border as shown

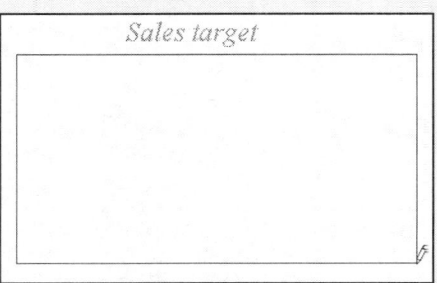

8 Drag to draw a vertical line as shown

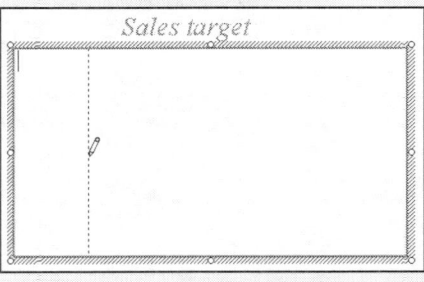

To create the first column in the table.

Add the remaining columns as shown

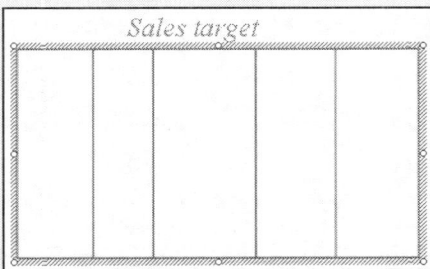

You should have five columns.

9 Drag to draw a horizontal line as shown

To create the first row in the table.

Add the remaining rows as shown

To turn off the Draw Table tool.

10 Click anywhere outside of the table on the slide

11 Add text as shown

Sales target				
Products	1st Qtr	2nd Qtr	3rd Qtr	4th Qtr
Cumin				
Cloves				
Basil Leaf				

12 Place the pointer over the border between the third and fourth columns

   Drag to the left to increase the width of the fourth column

13 Select the right border, and drag as shown

14 Place the pointer again over the right border, and double-click

   The fifth column is resized to fit the text.

   Resize the other columns to fit all the text

   If necessary.

15 Close the Tables and Borders toolbar

16 Update and close the presentation

Unit summary: Using organization charts and tables

Topic A In this topic, you learned how to use the **Organization Chart toolbar**. You learned that you can use the Organization Chart toolbar to **format an organization chart** in a presentation. You **rearranged** the boxes in an organization chart by applying a **style**. You also learned how to **modify** an organization chart by **formatting text, adding a border style**, and **adding a background color**.

Topic B In this topic, you learned how to **format** and **align text** in a table. You learned that you can **format** a table by changing its **fill color, border color**, and **border width**. You also learned how to **draw** a table by using the **Tables and Borders toolbar**.

Independent practice activity

1. Open Employee details.
2. Save the presentation as **My employee details**.
3. Move to the second slide.
4. Rearrange the second- and third-level boxes by applying the Right-Hanging layout style.
5. Fit the text for all the boxes.
6. Apply formatting of your choice to the text in the second-level boxes.
7. Add a border style to the third-level boxes.
8. Add a background color to the first-level box.
9. Add a new slide to the presentation. Apply the Title Only layout.
10. Type **Employee details** as the title of the slide.
11. Using the Tables and Borders toolbar, draw a table as shown in Exhibit 3-4.
12. Add text to the table as shown in Exhibit 3-5.
13. Format the text in the first row as Arial Narrow, 24pt, bold. Format the text in the second and third rows as Arial Narrow, 20pt, Italic.
14. Run the presentation.
15. Update and close the presentation.

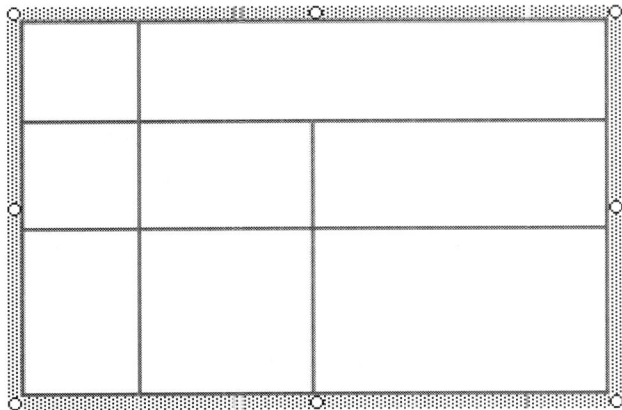

Exhibit 3-4: The table for Step 10 of the Independent Practice Activity

Name	Tom Wilkins	
Emp-Code	Emp-Status	Address
E002	Trainee	27 Sherry Lane Apt 253 New York City NY

Exhibit 3-5: The table after Step 11 of the Independent Practice Activity

Review questions

1 List the steps used to apply a new style to an organization chart.

2 What can you do to delineate the levels of your organization more clearly?

3 What toolbar can you use to change the style, width, and color of a table border? You can also use the Fill Color button on this toolbar to change a table's background color.

4 What dialog box can you use to change the border style and color of a table?

5 What technique can you use to automatically resize a column width to fit the text it contains?

Unit 4
Advanced presentation techniques

Unit time: 45 minutes

Complete this unit, and you'll know how to:

A Add action buttons to a presentation, and modify them.

B Create customized slide shows from a presentation, and edit them.

C Set up a review cycle for your presentations.

Topic A: Adding special effects

This topic covers the following Microsoft Office Specialist exam objective.

#	Objective
PP03S-4-2	Adding and modifying Action buttons

Adding action buttons

Explanation

You can insert action buttons to add interactivity to a presentation and give it a Web-browser-like interface. Action buttons help you scroll through a presentation. For example, on every slide, you can add a Home button, which, when clicked, takes you back to the first slide in the presentation. You can also add an End button, which takes you to the last slide. To add an action button, you must be in Master view.

To add an action button:

1 Switch to Master view.
2 Choose Slide Show, Action Buttons, and then select the action button from the menu.
3 On the slide, drag to create the action button. Releasing the mouse button opens the Action Settings dialog box, shown in Exhibit 4-1.
4 From the Hyperlink to list, select the target for the button. For example, if you are creating a Home button, you should select First Slide.
5 Click OK.

After adding the action button to the slide master, you can resize and reposition the button. You can also change its color, line style, and other format settings.

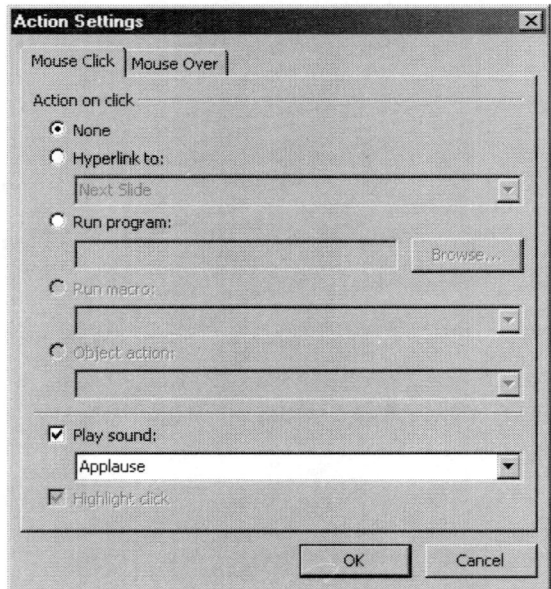

Exhibit 4-1: The Action Settings dialog box

Advanced presentation techniques

Adding action buttons with sound

You can add sound to an action button. When the presenter clicks the action button, the associated sound will play. To add an action button with sound, you must check the Play sound check box in the Action Settings dialog box and then select a sound from the drop-down list.

Do it!

A-1: Adding an action button with sound

Here's how	Here's why
1 Open Exotic spices	(From the current unit folder.) You'll add an action button with sound to this presentation.
2 Save the presentation as **My exotic spices**	
3 Switch to Master view	
4 Choose **Slide Show**, **Action Buttons**, as shown	
Select the indicated button	The pointer changes to a + shape.
5 Drag to create the action button as shown	The Action Settings dialog box opens when you release the mouse button.

6	Verify that the Mouse Click tab is activated	You'll use this tab to specify an action for the button.
	Under Action on click, select **Hyperlink to**	This helps you to set a target location for the action button.
	In the Hyperlink to list, verify that Next Slide is selected	To specify that clicking the action button will take you to the next slide in the presentation.
	Verify that Play sound is checked	If this option is not checked, you cannot access the Play sound drop-down list.
	From the Play sound list, select **Drum Roll**	To specify that the Drum Roll sound will play when you click the action button.
	Click **OK**	To apply the settings and to close the Action Settings dialog box.
7	Deselect the action button	
8	Switch to Normal view	
9	Run the slide show	
	Click the action button	To hear the drum roll and move to the next slide.
	Move through the presentation	Click the action button.
	Switch to Normal view	
10	Update the presentation	

Modifying an action button

Explanation

When you need to change the action settings of an action button, you use the Action Settings dialog box. For example, you can change the hyperlink and the sound applied to the button. To open the Action Settings dialog box, right-click the action button you want to modify and choose Action Settings.

Do it!

A-2: Modifying an action button

Here's how	Here's why
1 Switch to Master view	You'll change the sound applied to the action button.
2 Right-click the action button	To open a shortcut menu.
3 Choose **Action Settings...**	To open the Action Settings dialog box.
4 From the Play sound list, select **Breeze**	To specify that the breeze sound will play when you click the action button.
5 Click **OK**	To apply the settings and to close the Action Settings dialog box.
6 Switch to Normal view	
7 Run the slide show	
Click the action button	To hear the breeze sound and move to the next slide.
Move through the presentation	Click the action button.
Switch to Normal view	
8 Update the presentation	

Topic B: Working with slide show options

This topic covers the following Microsoft Office Specialist exam objective.

#	Objective
PP03S-4-2	Creating and editing custom shows

Creating custom slide shows

Explanation

PowerPoint provides several options for running a presentation, enabling you to set up slide shows that are based on the same presentation but adapted for different audiences. When you want to include only a few slides from a presentation in a slide show, you can create a custom slide show. To do this:

1. Choose Slide Show, Custom Shows to open the Custom Shows dialog box.
2. Click the New button to open the Define Custom Show dialog box.
3. In the Slide show name box, enter a name for the custom slide show.
4. From the Slides in presentation list, select a slide you want to include in the custom slide show. Then click the Add button.
5. For each additional slide you want to include, repeat step 4.
6. Click OK to close the Define Custom Show dialog box.
7. Click Show to close the Custom Shows dialog box and run the custom slide show.

Do it!

B-1: Creating a custom slide show

Here's how	Here's why
1 Choose **Slide Show, Custom Shows...**	To open the Custom Shows dialog box. Only the New and Close buttons are activated. This is because there are no existing custom shows to edit, remove, copy, or show.
2 Click **New**	To open the Define Custom Show dialog box.
3 In the Slide show name box, enter **Fast Moving Spices**	This will be the name of the custom show.
4 From the Slides in presentation list, select **4. Cinnamon**	You'll add this slide to your custom show.
Click **Add**	To add the fourth slide to your custom show.
5 Add slides 5 and 6 to the custom show	Select the slides, and click the Add button.
Click **OK**	To close the Define Custom Show dialog box. All the buttons are now active.

6 Click **Show**	To run the three-slide presentation.
7 Switch to Normal view	
8 Update the presentation	

Editing custom slide shows

Explanation

To edit a custom slide show:
1 Choose Slide Show, Custom to open the Custom Shows dialog box.
2 Select a custom show, and click Edit to open the Define Custom Show dialog box. You use this dialog box to add or remove slides from the custom slide show. You can also rearrange the order of slides.
3 Click OK to close the Define Custom Show dialog box.
4 Click Show to run the custom show you just edited.

Do it!

B-2: Editing a custom slide show

Here's how	Here's why
1 Choose **Slide Show, Custom Shows...**	To open the Custom Shows dialog box.
2 Verify that Fast Moving Spices is selected	
Click **Edit**	To open the Define Custom Show dialog box.
3 From the Slides in presentation list, select **3. Saffron**	
Click **Add**	To add a slide to the custom show.
4 From the Slides in custom show, select **3. Basil leaf**	
Click **Remove**	To remove the basil leaf slide from the custom show.
5 From the Slides in custom show, select **3. Saffron**	If necessary.
Click the up arrow	To move the slide up by one position.
Click **OK**	To close the Define Custom Show dialog box.
6 Click **Show**	To run the slide presentation.
7 Switch to Normal view	
8 Update and close the presentation	

Topic C: Setting up review cycles

This topic covers the following Microsoft Office Specialist exam objectives.

#	Objective
PP03S-3-1	Tracking, accepting and rejecting changes in a presentation
PP03S-3-2	Adding, editing and deleting comments in a presentation
PP03S-3-3	Comparing and merging presentations

What's a review cycle?

Explanation

In a work environment, you will most likely need to send your presentation out for other people to review. An easy way to do this is to set up a review cycle. A *review cycle* involves four main steps: sending a presentation for review, reviewing a presentation, accepting or rejecting changes, and ending a review. This cycle helps you get feedback and comments from multiple persons and incorporate these changes.

Starting review cycles

A review cycle begins with sending a presentation for review. You might want to send the presentation to one or several reviewers. To do this, you can send your presentation as an e-mail message by using Microsoft Outlook or any other e-mail application on your computer. When you use Microsoft Outlook, the changes each reviewer makes are automatically tracked. This tracking helps you manage and review the changes made by all the reviewers. If you use any other e-mail application, you save a copy of your presentation for each reviewer in a folder, and send the presentation to the respective reviewer by choosing File, Send To, Mail Recipient (as Attachment).

To send a presentation for review by using Microsoft Outlook:

1. Save the presentation in PowerPoint. Either include all linked files, or embed the files in the presentation.
2. Choose File, Send To, Mail Recipient (for Review) to open a new Message window. The presentation is already attached to the e-mail message and appears as an icon.
3. In the To box, enter the reviewer's e-mail address. You can send the presentation to multiple reviewers.
4. Click Send to send the e-mail.

To send a presentation for review by using other e-mail applications:

1. In PowerPoint, choose File, Save As to open the Save As dialog box. In the File name box, enter a suitable name for the presentation. (You might want to use a name that will indicate who is reviewing the presentation.) From the Save as type list, select Presentation for Review. Click Save.
2. Choose File, Send To, Mail Recipient, (as Attachment) to open a new Message window.
3. In the To box, enter the reviewer's e-mail address, and then click Send.

Do it!

C-1: Sending a presentation for review

Questions and answers

1 Why do you need to set up a review cycle?

2 How do you start a review cycle by using Microsoft Outlook?

3 How do you set up a review cycle if you are not using Microsoft Outlook?

Reviewing presentations

Explanation

If you are the person reviewing the presentation, you can review it in any version of PowerPoint. You can change the presentation and attach your comments by using the Insert Comment button on the Reviewing toolbar. When you make a change in a presentation, PowerPoint displays markups in the right margin to identify the change or comment.

To delete a comment or markup, click the down-arrow to the right of the Delete Comment button on the Reviewing toolbar. This displays a menu with delete choices. You can also use the Previous Item and Next Item buttons to view the inserted comments. These two buttons become available after the first comment is inserted.

To review a presentation:

1. Open the e-mail message containing the presentation.
2. Double-click the attachment to open the presentation in PowerPoint. The Reviewing toolbar, shown in Exhibit 4-2, becomes available.
3. Insert comments and make changes where necessary.
4. You can return the reviewed presentation by clicking the Reply with Changes button on the Reviewing toolbar. A new Message window opens with the reviewed presentation as an attachment.
5. In the To box, enter the sender's e-mail address. Click Send.

Exhibit 4-2: The Reviewing toolbar

Do it!

C-2: Reviewing and sending back a presentation

Questions and answers
1 How do you open a presentation to start reviewing it?
2 Which version of PowerPoint can you use to review a presentation?
3 How does a reviewer review a presentation?
4 How do you send the presentation back to the author?

Accepting and rejecting changes

Explanation

After you receive all the reviewed presentations, you'll want to open them and merge them with your original presentation. When you merge the presentations, the Revisions Pane becomes available with two tabs: Gallery and List. The Gallery tab displays the slides with the changes made by the reviewers, and the name of the reviewer appears above each slide. The List tab lists all the changes and comments. The list is color coded to distinguish between the changes made by different reviewers.

To accept or reject changes made by a reviewer:

1. Open the reviewed presentation from the message window. The presentation opens in PowerPoint, and a message box appears. The message tells you to merge the reviewed and original presentations. Click Yes.
2. The Revisions Pane becomes available. You can view the changes made in the Gallery tab, and view a list of changes in the List tab. Click the Apply or Unapply button to accept or reject the changes. The Apply and Unapply buttons are shown in Exhibit 4-3.
3. Click the End Review button to end the review cycle. After ending a review cycle, you cannot merge any more reviewed presentations with the original presentation.

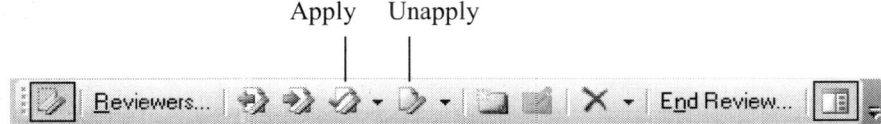

Exhibit 4-3: The Apply, Unapply, and End Review buttons on the Reviewing toolbar

Printing comments

You can also print reviewers' comments if you want to keep a hard copy of them for reference. To print the comments made by a reviewer:

1. Choose File, Print to open the Print dialog box.
2. From the Print what list, select Handouts or Notes Pages.
3. Check Print comments and ink markup.
4. Click OK to close the dialog box and print the comment pages.

Do it! **C-3: Completing a review cycle**

Questions and answers
1 How do you accept and review changes?
2 Three people reviewed your presentation. How will you distinguish between their changes and comments?
3 How does the review cycle end?
4 How can you print comment pages?

Unit summary: Advanced presentation techniques

Topic A In this topic, you learned how to **add** an **action button** to a presentation. You learned that to add an action button, you can choose **Slide Show, Action Buttons** and the action button. Then, you learned how to **modify** an action button.

Topic B In this topic, you learned how to show different versions of the same presentation by setting up different **slide shows**. After setting up a slide show, you learned how to **create a custom slide show** that includes only selected slides from a presentation. You also learned how to **edit** a **custom slide show**.

Topic C In this topic, you learned how to **set up** a **review cycle** by **sending a presentation** for review. Then you learned how to **review a presentation, accept and reject changes**, and **end a review**.

Independent practice activity

1. Open Benefits.
2. Save the presentation as **My benefits**.
3. Switch to Master view.
4. Add an action button that will display the previous slide when clicked.
5. Switch to Normal view.
6. Run the presentation.
7. Create a custom slide show that includes slides 1, 3, and 4 only. Name the custom show as **New Schemes**.
8. Run the custom slide show.
9. Update and close the presentation.

Review questions

1. What view must you be in before adding an action button?

2. How do you open the Action Settings dialog box for an action button?

3. List the steps used to edit a custom slide show.

4 When you review a presentation, how can you change it and attach your comments?

5 The Revisions Pane contains two tabs: Gallery and List. What do these tabs display?

Unit 5
Advanced presentation delivery options

Unit time: 50 minutes

Complete this unit, and you'll know how to:

A Broadcast a presentation by using Microsoft NetMeeting.

B Use the Shared Workspace task pane, and create a Document Workspace.

C Embed fonts in a presentation, compress pictures, and use the Package for CD feature to package and run a packaged presentation.

D Work with on-screen navigation tools, and annotate a slide.

Topic A: Online meetings

This topic covers the following Microsoft Office Specialist exam objective.

#	Objective
PP03S-4-5	Scheduling and defining settings for Online Broadcasts

Microsoft NetMeeting

Explanation

When you broadcast a presentation, you might want to interact with your viewers on multiple computers in different locations. The Microsoft NetMeeting feature helps you do this. For example, if you want to show a presentation to colleagues who work in offices located in various cities or countries, you can broadcast it by using Microsoft NetMeeting.

When you broadcast a presentation over the Web, you cannot interact directly with viewers. However, direct interaction with your audience is sometimes necessary. For example, say you're working on a project that requires you to share and discuss information with team members. Microsoft NetMeeting is useful in such situations. In this kind of broadcast, the presenter and all the participants need to have Microsoft NetMeeting installed on their computers.

A Microsoft NetMeeting broadcast is similar to a teleconference in that you begin by calling the participants directly. When you share a presentation over NetMeeting, all the participants can view the slide show by default, but they can't modify it. However, if you choose Allow Control, participants can also change the presentation.

To broadcast a presentation by using Microsoft NetMeeting:

1. Choose Start, Programs, Accessories, Communications, NetMeeting to open the Microsoft NetMeeting wizard. Follow the steps of the wizard. After you've entered the required information in the wizard, the NetMeeting dialog box opens.
2. Click the Place Call button to open the Place A Call dialog box. Enter the computer name or network address of the person you want to call. From the Using list, select an option.
3. Click the Call button. This will display the Microsoft NetMeeting notification box on the recipient's screen. For this to happen, Microsoft NetMeeting must be open on the recipient's computer.
4. To view the presentation, the recipient needs to click the Accept button. This open the Microsoft NetMeeting window.
5. Choose Tools, Sharing to open the Sharing dialog box.
6. In the Sharing dialog box, select the presentation that you want to run, and click Share.
7. To permit all participants to modify the presentation, you can choose Allow Control.
8. Click Close.

With NetMeeting, you can run a presentation instantly on demand, rather than according to a specified schedule. To broadcast your presentation instantly on demand, you need Microsoft NetMeeting 2.11 or later.

Advanced presentation delivery options

Do it!

A-1: Using Microsoft NetMeeting

Questions and answers

1 When you use Microsoft NetMeeting, you can directly interact with your viewers. True or false?

2 Can you use a Web browser to participate in a NetMeeting broadcast?

3 Which button permits a participant to change the presentation being broadcast?

Scheduling and defining online broadcasts

Explanation

You can reach a wider audience by broadcasting a presentation over the Web. You can broadcast your presentation, including live video and audio narration, using the PowerPoint 2003 presentation broadcast feature. This feature can be downloaded from the Microsoft Office Online Web site. You can also record and save your presentation for future on-demand viewing.

As a presenter, you'll need PowerPoint 2003, Microsoft Internet Explorer 5.1 or later, and an e-mail client, such as Microsoft Outlook. If you want to include live video and audio, you'll also need a video camera and a microphone. Your audience members will need a Web browser, Microsoft Internet Explorer 5.1 or later is recommended. If you're broadcasting to a group of 10 or more, you'll need a Microsoft Windows Media Server.

After you've downloaded the broadcast feature, you can open the Broadcast Settings dialog box. This dialog box contains a Presenter tab, which provides options for specifying the file location of the presentation, audio/video settings, and if you want speaker notes to be displayed during the broadcast. The dialog box also contains an Advanced tab, which provides options for selecting Microsoft Windows Media Server or chat server locations for your broadcast.

You can use Microsoft Outlook or another e-mail client to schedule, or invite, participants to an online broadcast. Your invitations are initiated from PowerPoint when you set up a broadcast.

Do it!

A-2: Discussing online broadcasts

Questions and answers

1 What feature is needed to run an online broadcast and where can you find this feature?

2 Describe some of the settings available in the Broadcast Settings dialog box.

3 What software is needed for scheduling an online broadcast?

Topic B: Working with shared workspaces

Explanation

A *shared workspace* is a Microsoft Windows SharePoint Services site where members of a team can share documents and exchange information about their projects. A SharePoint Services site can be:

- **A regular site** — A site that is published to a specific domain.
- **A Meeting Workspace site** — A site that helps you conduct online meetings with team members, and track the attendees, agenda, and decisions made in those meetings. You can create this site by using the Meeting Workspace task pane in Outlook 2003.
- **A Document Workspace site** — A site that helps you share documents and information, such as task assignments and deadlines. You can create a Document Workspace by using the Shared Workspace task pane in Office applications such as Word 2003, PowerPoint 2003, and Outlook 2003.

The Shared Workspace task pane

The Shared Workspace task pane displays information about the SharePoint Services sites. This information includes the participants of the workspace, the list of tasks, and the hyperlinks shared among team members. To display the Shared Workspace task pane (shown in Exhibit 5-1), open a PowerPoint presentation, and then choose Tools, Shared Workspace.

When you open a document—such as a Word document, an Excel worksheet, or a PowerPoint presentation—in a Document Workspace, the Shared Workspace task pane opens in the application. For example, when you open a PowerPoint presentation in a Document Workspace, the presentation opens in PowerPoint 2003 along with the Shared Workspace task pane.

You view the list of Document Workspace members and their online status by clicking the Members tab. You can also add new team members to the Document Workspace and define their roles if you have administrative rights. These are the roles you can assign to your team members:

- **Reader** — Has permission to read the documents in the Document Workspace.
- **Contributor** — Has permission to add content to the existing documents in the Document Workspace.
- **Web Designer** — Has permission to create lists and document libraries and to customize pages in the Web site.
- **Administrator** — Has full control over the Document Workspace.

Exhibit 5-1: A sample Shared Workspace task pane

The following table lists the various tabs available in the Shared Workspace task pane:

Tab	Description
Status	Displays the restrictions or errors in the document in a Document Workspace.
Members	Displays the names of the members who have the rights to access the site and their online status.
Tasks	Displays the tasks assigned to different members of the team.
Documents	Displays the documents in a Document Workspace.
Links	Displays the links available in a Document Workspace.
Document Information	Displays documentation information such as the creator of the document and the date when the document was last modified.

Advanced presentation delivery options

Do it!

B-1: Discussing the Shared Workspace task pane

Questions and answers

1 What is a shared workspace?

2 You can open a SharePoint Services site by using a Web browser. True or false?

3 In the Shared Workspace task pane, the _____ tab displays the Document Workspace restrictions.

4 In the Shared Workspace task pane, you can view the online status of the members of a Document Workspace. True or false?

5 Using the Shared Workspace task pane, you can add new documents to your Document Workspace. True or false?

Creating Document Workspaces

Explanation

You can use the Shared Workspace task pane in PowerPoint 2003 or use Microsoft Outlook 2003 to create a Document Workspace. For this, you should have the permission to create a Document Workspace in the Microsoft Windows SharePoint Services site.

Using the Shared Workspace task pane

To create a Document Workspace by using the Shared Workspace task pane:
1. Open the presentation in Microsoft PowerPoint 2003.
2. Choose Tools, Shared Workspace to open the Shared Workspace task pane.
3. In the Location for new workspace box, enter the Web address of the SharePoint server.
4. Click the Create button in the Shared Workspace task pane.

Using Microsoft Outlook 2003

To create a Document Workspace by using Microsoft Outlook 2003:
1. Open Microsoft Outlook 2003.
2. Choose File, New, Mail Message to open a new Message window.
3. In the To box, enter the e-mail address of the person who wants to be a member of the Document Workspace.
4. In the Cc box, enter the e-mail address of other members who are part of the team.
5. In the Subject box, enter the subject of the message. Type the message in the message area of the new Message window.
6. Choose Insert, File to open the Insert File dialog box.
7. Select the document you want to add to your Document Workspace, and click the Insert button.
8. Click Attachment Options to display the Attachment Options task pane.
9. Under Send attachments as in the Attachment Options task pane, select Shared attachments.
10. In the Create Document Workspace at box, enter the Web address of the Microsoft Windows SharePoint Services site. Then click Send on the Standard toolbar.

Do it! **B-2: Creating a Document Workspace**

Questions and answers

1 You can create a Document Workspace by using Microsoft Outlook 2003. True or false?

2 You need permission to create a Document Workspace in the Microsoft Windows SharePoint Services site. True or false?

3 Name the task pane used to create a Document Workspace.

Topic C: Working with the Package for CD feature

This topic covers the following Microsoft Office Specialist exam objectives.

#	Objective
PP03S-4-5	Packaging presentations to folders for storage on a Compact Disc (e.g., Package for CD)
PP03S-4-6	Creating and using folders for presentation storage (This objective is also covered in *PowerPoint 2003: Basic*, in the unit titled "Building new presentations.")

Why "Package for CD"?

Explanation

If you want to run your presentation on a computer other than your own—for example, while you are on a business trip—you can use PowerPoint's Package for CD feature to copy and transport your files on a CD. Before using the Package for CD feature, compress all the pictures and embed all the fonts used in the presentation. When you compress a picture, its file size is reduced. Embedding fonts is necessary to ensure that the text in your presentation appears correctly. You can embed only copyrighted fonts. TrueType fonts with built-in copyright restrictions cannot be embedded.

The Package for CD feature keeps all related presentation files together while compressing them for a more efficient transfer. This feature is also useful when you want to move all your presentations to a different computer, such as when you're moving to a new office. You can use PowerPoint Viewer to show your presentation if the new computer does not have PowerPoint installed.

Embedding TrueType fonts

Embedding TrueType fonts is useful when you have distinctive fonts in your presentation and you need to run the presentation on a computer that doesn't have these fonts installed. However, embedding fonts increases the file size of the presentation. You can minimize the file size by embedding only those font characters that are used in the presentation. But if you're sending the presentation to another person for review, you have to embed the entire font set to enable the reviewer to make changes.

To embed a font in a presentation:

1. Choose File, Save As to open the Save As dialog box.
2. Click Tools to open the Tools menu.
3. Choose Save Options to open the Save Options dialog box.
4. Check Embed TrueType fonts.
5. Click OK, and then save the presentation.

Do it!

C-1: Embedding TrueType fonts in a presentation

Here's how	Here's why
1 Open Presentation	From the current unit folder.
2 Choose **File, Save As...**	To open the Save As dialog box.
3 Click **Tools**	To open the Tools menu.
Choose **Save Options...**	To open the Save Options dialog box.
4 Check **Embed TrueType fonts**	To embed all the TrueType fonts used in the presentation.
Click **OK**	
5 Save the presentation as **My presentation**	

Compressing pictures

Explanation

Pictures and images are made up of tiny dots. The clarity of a picture depends on the number of dots that make up the picture. This is called the *resolution*, which is measured by counting the number of dots per inch (dpi). The file size of a picture depends on its resolution. If the resolution of a picture is high, its file size is also high.

In PowerPoint, you can reduce the file size of a picture by reducing its resolution to 96 dpi for the Web and 200 dpi for print. Deleting any cropped areas of pictures also helps reduce file size. Cropped pictures are pictures that have been resized to show only a part of the picture. You need to check Delete cropped areas of pictures in the Compress Pictures dialog box to delete cropped areas of pictures.

To compress and reduce the file size of a picture:

1. Select one or all the pictures in your presentation.
2. Click Compress Pictures on the Picture toolbar to open the Compress Pictures dialog box.
3. Under Change Resolution, select Web/Screen or Print.
4. Under Options, check Compress pictures and Delete cropped areas of pictures.
5. Click OK.

Advanced presentation delivery options **5–13**

Do it! **C-2: Compressing a picture**

Here's how	Here's why
1 Move to the last slide	
2 Select the picture	The Picture toolbar becomes visible.
3 Click [button]	(The Compress Pictures button is on the Picture toolbar.) To open the Compress Pictures dialog box.
4 Under Change resolution, select **Web/Screen**	To change the picture resolution to 96 dpi. The effect will not be visible on the screen. The difference in file size can be observed while packaging a presentation (with several pictures) with and without compressing pictures.
5 Under Options, verify that Compress pictures is checked	To compress the pictures.
6 Click **OK**	
	A message box appears, stating that compressing pictures might reduce the quality of your images.
Click **Apply**	
Deselect the picture	
7 Update the presentation	

Packaging and running presentations

Explanation

You package a presentation by using the Package for CD feature. Sometimes, the destination computer (the computer on which you want to run a packaged presentation) might not have PowerPoint installed. So, it's useful to package your presentation along with PowerPoint Viewer, which enables you to run a presentation on a computer that doesn't have PowerPoint installed. However, when you use Viewer, you cannot modify the presentation. If the packaged presentation is on a CD, then when you insert the CD into the CD-ROM drive, the presentation will run automatically.

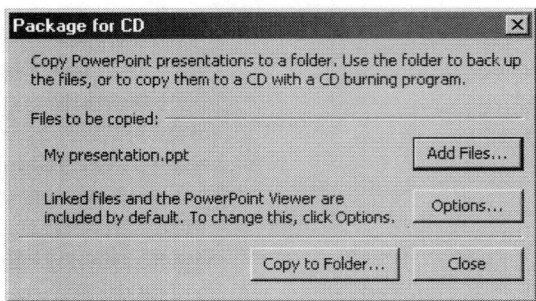

Exhibit 5-2: The Package for CD dialog box

Do it!

C-3: Packaging and running a presentation

Here's how	Here's why
1 Choose **File, Package for CD...**	To open the Package for CD dialog box, as shown in Exhibit 5-2.
2 Click **Options**	To open the Options dialog box.
3 Clear **Linked files**	This option is not necessary because the current presentation does not contain any linked files.
Check **Embedded TrueType fonts**	To embed all the TrueType fonts used in this presentation.
Click **OK**	To close the Options dialog box and return to the Package for CD dialog box.
4 Click **Copy to Folder**	To open the Copy to Folder dialog box.
Verify that the Folder name box reads PresentationCD	
Click **Browse**	You'll specify a path to save the packaged presentation.
Navigate to the current unit folder, and double-click **Packaging**	To open the Packaging folder.
Click **Select**	To return to the Copy to Folder dialog box. You'll package the presentation in this folder.

Advanced presentation delivery options 5–15

5	Click **OK**	The Location box has the name of the current folder. A status box appears, showing the progress of file compression.
6	Click **Close**	To close the Package for CD dialog box.
7	Update and close the presentation	
8	Choose **Start**, **Programs**, **Accessories**, **Windows Explorer**	To open Windows Explorer.
9	Navigate to the Packaging folder in the current unit folder	
	Double-click **PresentationCD**	To open the PresentationCD folder. The pptview application file in the folder can be used to view the presentation on computers without PowerPoint.
10	Double-click **pptview**	To view the packaged presentation. The Microsoft Office PowerPoint Viewer dialog box appears.
	If the Microsoft Licensing Agreement screen appears, click **Accept**	If the Microsoft Licensing Agreement screen does not appear, skip this step.
	Verify that PresentationCD is selected in the Look in list	
11	Select **My presentation**	You'll run this presentation.
12	Click **Open**	The presentation slide show starts running.
	View the presentation	At the end of the slide show, the Microsoft Office PowerPoint Viewer dialog box appears.
13	Click **Cancel**	To close the Microsoft PowerPoint Viewer dialog box.
	Close Windows Explorer	

Topic D: Advanced delivery techniques

This topic covers the following Microsoft Office Specialist exam objective.

#	Objective
PP03S-4-4	Using pens, highlighters, arrows and pointers for emphasis

On-screen navigation

Explanation

You can scroll through a presentation in Slide Show view by using the mouse or the keyboard. When using the mouse, you can activate a special navigation tool called the Show Popup menu, shown in Exhibit 5-3. This menu provides several options for moving through slides. You display the Show Popup menu by right-clicking anywhere on the screen. You can also display the menu by clicking the Show Popup menu button in the lower-right corner of the screen.

To use the Show Popup menu:
1 Run the slide show.
2 Right-click to display the Show Popup menu.
3 Select an option.

Exhibit 5-3: The Show Popup menu

Navigating through slides

One of the most useful features of the Show Popup menu is the Go to Slide option. This option helps you move through slides in any order. To use this option:
1 Run the slide show.
2 Right-click to display the Show Popup menu.
3 Choose Go to Slide.
4 From the Slide titles list, select the slide to which you want to move.

Advanced presentation delivery options **5–17**

Do it! **D-1: Using the Show Popup menu during a slide show**

Here's how	Here's why
1 Maximize PowerPoint	(If necessary.) Click the Microsoft PowerPoint button on the taskbar.
2 Open Celebration	
3 Save the presentation as **My celebration**	
4 Run the presentation	
5 Click the Show Popup menu button as shown	
	(In the lower-left corner of the screen.) To display the Show Popup menu. You can also right-click to display the Show Popup menu, but it's different from the menu obtained by clicking the Show Popup menu button. The menu obtained by the using the Show Popup menu button does not have the Pointer Options command.
6 Choose **Go to Slide**	
Select as shown	
	To move to slide 5.
7 Display the Show Popup menu	
Choose **End Show**	To end the slide show and return to Normal view.
8 Update the presentation	

Annotating a slide

Explanation

When you run a presentation, you might want to draw attention to a specific point on a slide. By using Ballpoint Pen, Felt Tip Pen, or Highlighter, you can annotate a presentation while it's running. For example, you can use Ballpoint Pen to underline or circle a key point on a slide.

To activate Ballpoint Pen, display the Show Popup menu and choose Pointer Options, Ballpoint Pen. The mouse pointer changes to a dot, which you can drag to draw on your slides. Even when Ballpoint Pen is activated, you can use the mouse to scroll through the slide show. To do so, click the Show Popup menu button, choose Go to Slide, and select the slide you want to view. When the new slide appears, the mouse pointer will still be in Ballpoint Pen mode. To change the ink color, display the Show Popup menu, choose Pointer Options, Ink Color, and then select an ink color. To turn off Ballpoint Pen, press the Esc key.

To erase the lines you've drawn on a slide, choose Pointer Options, Erase All Ink on Slide. You can also choose Pointer Options, Eraser to erase selected annotations. At the end of the slide show, a message appears asking you whether to annotate the slides so you can view them while editing. Click Keep to apply the changes.

Exhibit 5-4: The annotated slide after Step 6

Advanced presentation delivery options **5-19**

Do it! **D-2: Using Ballpoint Pen**

Here's how	Here's why
1 Run the slide show	
2 Go to the last slide	Right-click, choose Go to Slide, 6 Slide 6.
3 Right-click anywhere on the screen	To display the Show Popup menu. If you use the Show Popup menu button to display the Show Popup menu, the Pointer Options option will not be available.
Choose **Pointer Options, Ballpoint Pen**	The shape of the pointer changes to a red dot.
4 Drag to draw a circle around **Celebration!**	As shown in Exhibit 5-4. The default color of the ink is red.
5 Display the Show Popup menu	(Right-click anywhere on the screen.) You'll change the color of the ink.
Choose **Pointer Options, Ink Color**	
Select the blue ink as shown	
6 Draw a line under the first bullet	As shown in Exhibit 5-4. Notice that the color of the ink has changed.
Press `ESC`	To change the pointer to an arrow.
7 Display the Show Popup menu	
Choose **Pointer Options, Erase All Ink on Slide**	To erase your annotations.
8 Click as shown	
	To display a popup menu.
Choose **Arrow Options, Hidden**	To hide the pointer arrow.

9	Press `PAGE UP`	To move to the previous slide. The pointer is invisible.
10	Right-click on the screen	To display the Show Popup menu.
	Choose **Pointer options, Arrow Options, Visible**	To unhide the arrow.
	Press `ESC`	To end the slide show.
11	Update and close the presentation	

Unit summary: Advanced presentation delivery options

Topic A In this topic, you learned how to **broadcast a presentation on demand** by using **Microsoft NetMeeting**.

Topic B In this topic, you learned how to use the **Shared Workspace task pane** and create a **Document Workspace**.

Topic C In this topic, you learned how to package a presentation by using the **Package for CD feature**. You also learned how to run a packaged presentation.

Topic D In this topic, you learned how to use the on-screen navigation tools and how to annotate a slide.

Independent practice activity

1 Open Packaging.

2 Package the presentation into the Practice packaging folder in the current unit folder. Embed the fonts, and do not include linked files.

3 In the fourth slide, underline the last line by using the Ballpoint Pen tool.

4 Erase all the ink on the slide.

5 Close the presentation.

Review questions

1 What feature will you need if you want to broadcast your presentation over the Web and provide direct interaction with your audience, much like a teleconference?

2 When using the PowerPoint 2003 online broadcast feature, your broadcast invitations are initiated from your e-mail client. True or False?

3 What is a shared workspace?

4 Which feature would you use to distribute a presentation via CD?

5 When packaging a presentation for CD, how can you ensure that destination computers will be able to play the presentation? (Destination computers might not have PowerPoint installed.)

Unit 6
Customizing the environment

Unit time: 40 minutes

Complete this unit, and you'll know how to:

A Customize and create toolbars.

B Automate your work by creating and running macros.

Topic A: Customizing and creating toolbars

Explanation

When you create a new blank presentation, PowerPoint displays three toolbars: Standard, Formatting, and Drawing. You can customize these and other toolbars to suit your work style, or you can create your own toolbar.

Customizing toolbars

As you work in PowerPoint, you might find that you don't use some of the default toolbar buttons. At the same time, you might frequently use commands that do not appear as buttons on any toolbar. To speed up your work, you can customize toolbars by removing and adding buttons. For example, when using drawing objects, you might find that you duplicate objects frequently. With that in mind, you can add the Duplicate button to the Drawing toolbar.

To customize a toolbar:

1 Ensure that the toolbar you want to customize is visible. If it's hidden, choose View, Toolbars, and choose the toolbar from the submenu.
2 Choose Tools, Customize to open the Customize dialog box.
3 Click the Commands tab to view the options, shown in Exhibit 6-1.
4 From the Categories list, select the category to display the associated commands in the Commands list.
5 From the Commands list, drag the required command to the toolbar.
6 Click the Close button to close the Customize dialog box.

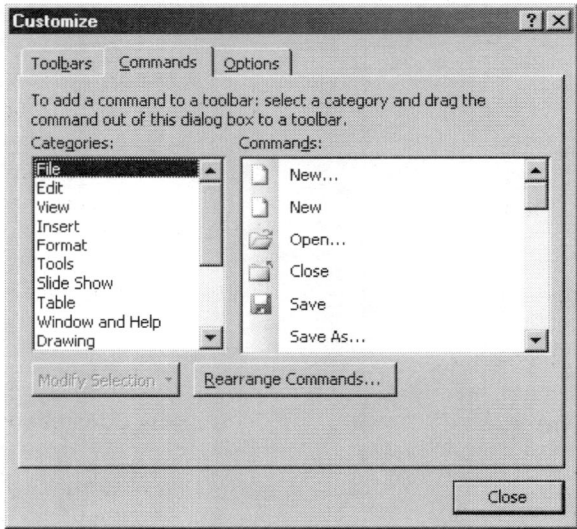

Exhibit 6-1: The Commands tab of the Customize dialog box

Do it!

A-1: Customizing a toolbar

Here's how	Here's why
1 Open Expansion	(From the current unit folder.) With this presentation open, you'll customize the Standard toolbar. The customized toolbar will then be available for all presentations.
2 Save the presentation as **My expansion**	
3 Choose **Tools, Customize...**	To open the Customize dialog box.
4 Click the **Commands** tab	If necessary.
From the Categories list, select **Edit**	To display the Edit command options in the Commands list.
5 From the Commands list, drag **Clear** to the Standard toolbar as shown	To add the Clear button to the toolbar. The shape of the mouse pointer changes when you start dragging.
Observe the Standard toolbar	The Clear button now appears between the Cut and Copy buttons on the Standard toolbar.
6 Add the Duplicate command to the Drawing toolbar	Scroll down in the Commands list to find the Duplicate command, and then drag it to the Drawing toolbar.
7 Click **Close**	To close the Customize dialog box.
8 Move to the second slide	
9 Select the oval	You'll duplicate this object.
Click	(The Duplicate button is now on the Drawing toolbar.) To duplicate the object.
10 Select the line	
Click	

6–4 PowerPoint 2003: Advanced

11	Position the objects as shown	
	Type text as shown	
12	Select **Kiosk**	(In the rectangle.) You'll edit this text.
	Click [eraser icon]	(The Clear button is on the Standard toolbar.) To clear the text.
	Type **Target locations**	
13	Update the presentation	

Creating toolbars

Explanation

You can create your own toolbars in PowerPoint. Creating a new toolbar is useful when you frequently use buttons that don't fall into any of the default toolbar categories. For example, you might want to create a Template toolbar that includes various template command buttons.

To create a toolbar:

1. Choose Tools, Customize to open the Customize dialog box.
2. Click the Toolbars tab (if necessary).
3. Click the New button to open the New Toolbar dialog box.
4. In the Toolbar name box, enter a name for the toolbar.
5. Click OK to close the New Toolbar dialog box. The new toolbar appears next to the Customize dialog box.
6. Drag the new toolbar to a location of your choice.
7. Click the Commands tab. Using the Categories list and the Commands list, add the command buttons of your choice to the new toolbar (by dragging).
8. Close the Customize dialog box.

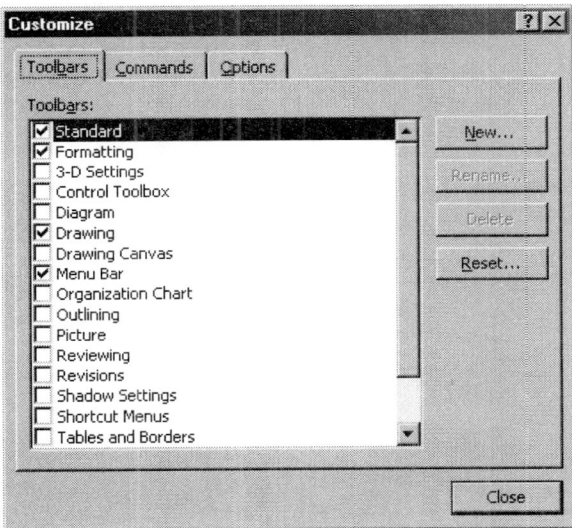

Exhibit 6-2: The Toolbars tab of the Customize dialog box

Do it! **A-2: Creating a toolbar**

Here's how	Here's why
1 Open the Customize dialog box	Choose Tools, Customize.
2 Click the **Toolbars** tab	(If necessary.) To view the options, as shown in Exhibit 6-2.
3 Click **New**	To open the New Toolbar dialog box.
Edit the Toolbar name box to read **Special**	This will be the name of your toolbar.
Click **OK**	To close the New Toolbar dialog box.
4 Observe the toolbar	
5 Drag the Special toolbar below the Formatting toolbar as shown	
6 Click the **Commands** tab	
7 From the Categories list, select **Format**	To display the Format command options in the Commands list.
8 Add the Slide Design command to the Special toolbar	You'll have to scroll down in the Commands list to find the Slide Design command.
9 From the Categories list, select **Insert**	To view the Insert command options in the Commands list.
Add the From File command to the Special toolbar	
	You'll have to scroll down in the Commands list to find the From File command.
10 Click **Close**	To close the Customize dialog box.
11 Click	(The Slide Design button is on the Special toolbar.) To display the Slide Design task pane. You'll apply a different design template to the presentation.
Select as shown	
	(Scroll down the task pane.) To apply this design template. The appearance of the presentation changes to reflect the new template.

12	Add a new Title Only slide	
	In the Title placeholder, type **Kiosks**	
13	Click [icon]	(The From File button is on the Special toolbar.) To open the Insert Picture dialog box. You'll insert a picture from a file.
	From the Files of type list, select **All Files**	
	Select **Kiosk**	From the current unit folder.
	Click **Insert**	To add the selected picture.
	Resize the picture	Make it larger so you can view the picture clearly.
14	Update the presentation	

Topic B: Automating your work

Explanation

A *macro* is a series of commands that you can execute automatically with a single command. You can use macros to automate complex or repetitive tasks.

Creating macros

If you need to perform a series of time-consuming steps repeatedly, you might want to create a macro. For example, every time you insert the logo for the upcoming company picnic, you might find yourself performing the steps to open the WordArt Gallery, select a WordArt style, edit the text, size the logo, format the logo, and position the logo. To save time, you can create a macro that will perform all these steps automatically. This will also give your object a consistent look across all presentations.

To create a macro:

1. Choose Tools, Macro, Record New Macro to open the Record Macro dialog box.
2. Enter a name and a description for the macro.
3. Click OK to close the Record Macro dialog box and start recording the macro. The Stop Recording toolbar appears.
4. Perform the actions you want to include in the macro. As you work, PowerPoint records the sequence of steps.
5. When you have finished, click the Stop Recording button on the Stop Recording toolbar.

Do it!

B-1: Creating a macro

Here's how	Here's why
1 Move to the first slide	You'll create a macro.
2 Choose **Tools, Macro, Record New Macro...**	To open the Record Macro dialog box.
3 Edit the Macro name box to read **Logo**	This will be the name of the macro.
Verify that the Store macro in box contains My expansion	The macro will be stored in this presentation.
In the Description box, edit the text to read **This macro creates the Project Expansion logo**	To add a description of the macro.
Click **OK**	To close the Record Macro dialog box and begin recording the macro. Notice that the Stop Macro toolbar appears.
4 Click ![A]	(The Insert WordArt button is on the Drawing toolbar.) To open the WordArt Gallery dialog box.

Customizing the environment   **6–9**

5 Select the WordArt style as shown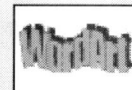

   Click **OK**   To open the Edit WordArt Text dialog box.

6 Edit the text to read
   Project Expansion

   Click **OK**   To apply the WordArt style.

7 Click [icon]   (The Format WordArt button is on the WordArt toolbar.) To open the Format WordArt dialog box.

   Click the **Colors and Lines** tab   If necessary.

   Under Fill, from the Color list, select an orange color

   Click **OK**   To change the color of the logo to orange.

8 Resize and position the logo as shown

   Deselect the logo   If necessary.

9 Click [icon]   (The Stop Recording button is on the Stop Recording toolbar.) To stop the macro recording.

10 Update the presentation

Running macros

Explanation

After you've created a macro, you can run it to accomplish the recorded task. To run a macro:

1 Choose Tools, Macro, Macros to open the Macro dialog box, shown in Exhibit 6-3.
2 Select the macro that you want to run.
3 Click the Run button to run the macro.

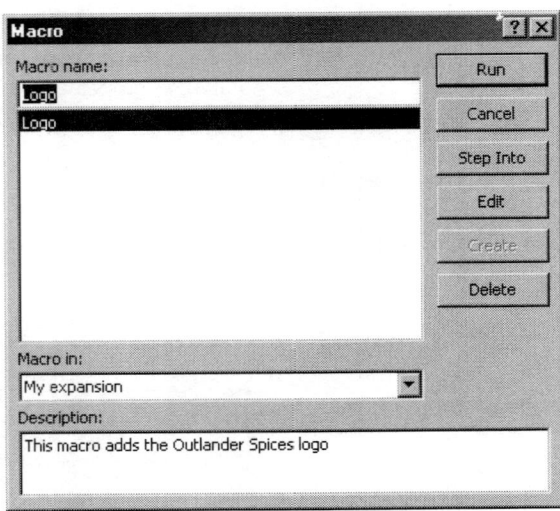

Exhibit 6-3: The Macro dialog box

Do it!

B-2: Running a macro

Here's how	Here's why
1 Move to the second slide	You'll run the Logo macro in this slide.
2 Choose **Tools, Macro, Macros...**	To open the Macro dialog box.
3 Under Macro name, verify that Logo is selected	You'll run this macro.
4 Click **Run**	To run the macro. Notice that the WordArt logo is inserted at the bottom of the slide.
5 Move to the third slide	You'll run the Logo macro in this slide.
6 Run the macro **Logo**	
7 Update and close the presentation	

Unit summary: Customizing the environment

Topic A — In this topic, you learned how to **customize a toolbar** by **removing** and **adding** buttons. You also learned how to **create a toolbar** to suit your needs.

Topic B — In this topic, you learned to how to **automate** complex tasks by **creating** and **running** a **macro**. You learned that you can create and run a macro by using the **Record Macro dialog box** and the **Macro dialog box**.

Independent practice activity

1. Create a new, blank presentation (use the Title Only layout).
2. Customize the Drawing toolbar by adding the Increase Indent button (in the Format category) and the Draw Table button (in the Table category).
3. Create a new toolbar named **My toolbar**, containing the Equation Editor and Record Sound buttons. (These buttons are in the Insert category.)
4. Dock the new toolbar below the Formatting toolbar.
5. Create a macro named **MyArt** that automatically inserts WordArt. (Create a WordArt with the text **The hottest spices!!!** and the formatting of your choice.) (*Hint*: There is no space in "MyArt".)
6. Add a new slide to the presentation. Change the layout to Title Only layout, and then run the macro on the new slide.
7. On your new toolbar, add a button that runs the MyArt macro. (*Hint:* In the Customize dialog box, click the Commands tab, and then choose Macros from the Categories list.)
8. Add a new slide, and then click the MyArt macro button to verify that it works correctly.
9. Save the presentation as **Practice presentation** in the current unit folder.
10. Close the presentation.

Review questions

1. When you create a presentation, which three toolbars are displayed automatically?

2. You can customize only the Standard, Formatting, and Drawing toolbars. True or False?

3. What dialog box would you use to create a toolbar and how do you open this dialog box?

4 What is a macro?

5 List the steps used to run a macro.

Unit 7
Microsoft Office integration

Unit time: 60 minutes

Complete this unit, and you'll know how to:

A Insert an Excel worksheet into a PowerPoint presentation, and edit the worksheet.

B Create PowerPoint slides based on a Word outline, insert a Word table into a presentation, send and edit a presentation in Word, and save a presentation as an RTF outline.

Topic A: Working with Excel

This topic covers the following Microsoft Office Specialist exam objective.

#	Objective
PP03S-1-2	Importing text from other sources (This objective is also covered in Topic B.)

Inserting worksheets

Explanation

While creating a presentation in PowerPoint, you might want to insert an Excel worksheet into a slide. You do this by embedding or linking the worksheet. When you import an object from one application into another, the two files involved are called the *source* and *destination* files. The Excel worksheet is the source file, and the PowerPoint presentation is the destination file.

Linking versus embedding a file

If you link the destination file to the source file, the PowerPoint slide displaying the worksheet is automatically updated when you modify the worksheet in Excel. However, the worksheet itself is not actually saved as part of the presentation.

Another option is to embed the source file in the destination file. In this case, the embedded worksheet is saved as part of the destination file. As a result, any changes made in the embedded worksheet in PowerPoint are reflected only in the destination file, not in the source file. At the same time, any changes made in the source file in Excel are not reflected in the presentation.

To insert an Excel worksheet into a presentation:

1. Choose Insert, Object to open the Insert Object dialog box.
2. Select Create from file, and then click the Browse button to open the Browse dialog box.
3. Select the Excel file, and click OK.
4. If you want to link the worksheet, check the Link check box. If you want to embed the worksheet, clear the Link check box.
5. Click OK.

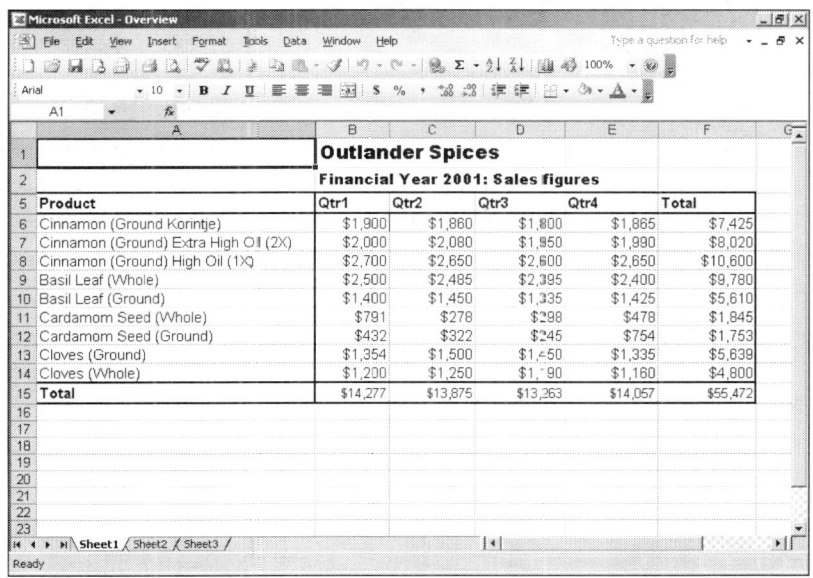

Exhibit 7-1: A sample Excel worksheet

Do it!

A-1: Inserting a worksheet

Here's how	Here's why
1 Open Project overview	(From the current unit folder.) You'll insert the Excel worksheet shown in Exhibit 7-1 into this presentation.
2 Save the presentation as **My project overview**	
3 Move to the second slide	You'll add a new slide.
4 Insert a new slide	Click the New Slide button on the Formatting toolbar.
Select the Title and Content layout	From the Slide Layout task pane.
Change the title of the slide to **Sales status**	As the title of the slide.
5 Choose **Insert**, **Object…**	To open the Insert Object dialog box.
Observe the dialog box	You can create a new object by specifying an object type, or you can insert an existing object by selecting Create from file.
6 Select **Create from file**	The Object type list is replaced by a File box, a Browse button, and a Link check box. The Link check box is disabled.
Click **Browse**	To open the Browse dialog box.
7 Select **Overview**	(From the current unit folder.) You'll insert this Excel worksheet into the current slide.
Click **OK**	To close the Browse dialog box. The Link check box is enabled.
8 Verify that the Link check box is cleared	To specify that the worksheet will be embedded rather than linked.
Click **OK**	To insert the worksheet into the slide. This might take a few moments to load.

Microsoft Office integration

9 Double-click the worksheet	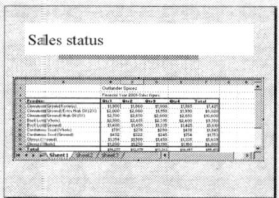	
		The worksheet opens in edit mode.
Resize the worksheet window as shown	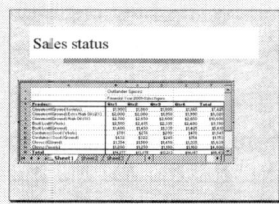	
		The empty columns should not be visible.
Click outside the worksheet		To return to Normal view.
10 Resize and position the worksheet as shown	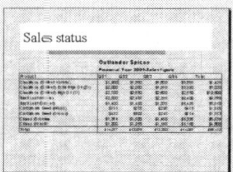	
		To enlarge the worksheet and make the contents readable. The resized worksheet might take a few moments to load.
11 Update the presentation		

Editing embedded worksheets

Explanation

After embedding an Excel worksheet in a slide, you might want to edit it. Keep in mind, however, that any changes you make in an embedded worksheet will not be reflected in the source file.

To edit an embedded worksheet:

1. Select the embedded worksheet.
2. Choose Edit, Worksheet Object, Edit. The PowerPoint interface changes to include components of Excel.
3. Select the cell you want to edit, and enter the new value.
4. Deselect the worksheet.

You can also change the background fill and line style of the worksheet in your presentation. To do this:

1. Select the embedded worksheet.
2. Choose Format, Object to open the Format Object dialog box.
3. Click the Colors and Lines tab, if necessary.
4. Select a background fill and line style.
5. Click OK to apply the changes.
6. Deselect the worksheet.

Do it!

A-2: Editing an embedded worksheet

Here's how	Here's why
1 Right-click the worksheet	To display a shortcut menu.
2 Choose **Worksheet Object, Edit**	To open the worksheet in an Excel window so that you can change it.
3 Observe cell B15	The current total for is Qtr1 $14,277.
Select cell B6	You'll enter a new value in this cell and observe the effect of this change.
4 Type **2000**	To change the value in cell B6 to $2,000.
5 Press ⏎ ENTER	
Observe cell B15	The total recalculates automatically, increasing to $14,377.
6 Minimize PowerPoint	

7	Choose **Start**, **Programs**, **Microsoft Office**, **Microsoft Office Excel 2003**	To open Microsoft Excel.
8	Click [icon]	(The Open button is on the Standard toolbar.) To display the Open dialog box.
	Select **Overview**	From the current unit folder.
	Click **Open**	To open the Excel file.
9	Observe cell B6 and cell B15	These cells do not reflect the changes made in PowerPoint.
10	Close Microsoft Excel	If prompted to save the changes, click No.
	Maximize PowerPoint	If necessary.
11	Select cells A5 through F5	You'll change the color of the labels in this row.
12	Click the down arrow next to the Font Color button	(The Font Color button is on the Formatting toolbar.) To display the color palette.
	Select a blue color	You can choose any shade of blue.
13	Deselect the worksheet	The column headings are now blue.
14	Right-click the worksheet	
	Choose **Format Object...**	To open the Format Object dialog box.
15	Click the **Colors and Lines** tab	If necessary.
	Under Fill, in the Color list, select the white color	To change the background color of the worksheet to white.
	Under Line, in the Color list, select a blue color	To add a blue border around the worksheet.
	Click **OK**	To close the Format Object dialog box.
16	Update the presentation	

Topic B: Working with Word

This topic covers the following Microsoft Office Specialist exam objectives.

#	Objective
PP03S-1-2	Importing text from other sources (This objective is also covered in Topic A.)
PP03S-4-8	Sending presentations to Microsoft Word

Examining Word outlines

Explanation

You can use an outline created in Word to create a PowerPoint presentation. Word outlines are formatted with different heading styles for each level, such as the Heading 1 style for level 1 and the Heading 2 style for level 2, as shown in Exhibit 7-2. You can apply these styles by using Word's Outlining toolbar. You can also collapse or expand different parts of an outline to show only the text in which you are interested.

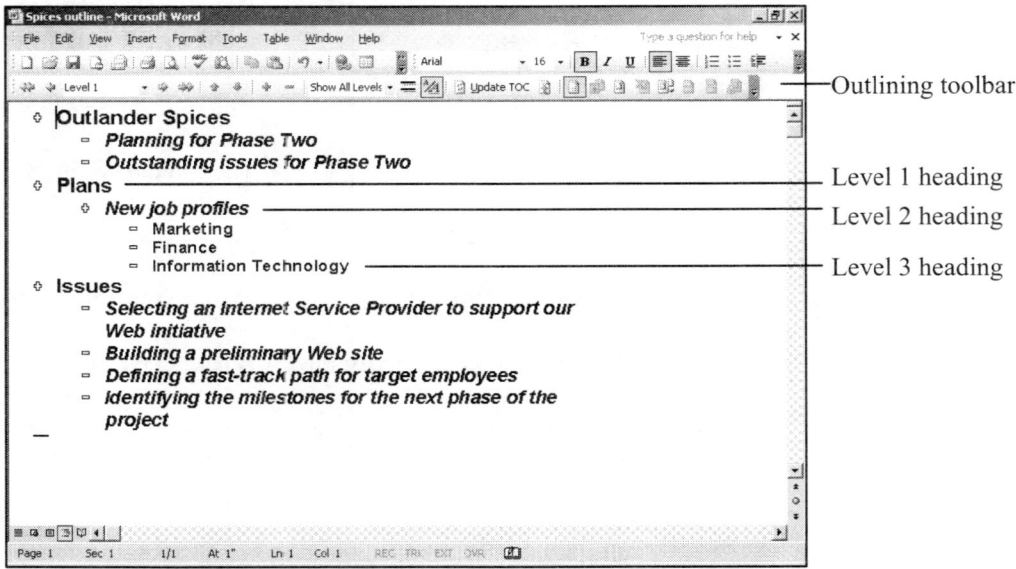

Exhibit 7-2: A sample Word outline

Do it!

B-1: Examining a Word outline

Here's how	Here's why
1 Minimize PowerPoint	You'll open Word and examine a document in Outline view.
2 Choose **Start**, **Programs**, **Microsoft Office**, **Microsoft Office Word 2003**	To start Microsoft Word.
3 In the Getting Started task pane, under Open, click **Open**	To display the Open dialog box.
Select **Spices outline**	From the current unit folder.
Click **Open**	To open the document.
4 Observe the Outlining toolbar	The Outlining toolbar appears just above the document window, as shown in Exhibit 7-2.
5 Select **Show Level 1** as shown	(On the Outlining toolbar.) To show only the level-1 text in the outline. The text collapses to show only level-1 headings: Outlander Spices, Plans, and Issues.
6 Select **Show Level 3**	(On the Outlining toolbar.) To show levels 1, 2, and 3. The outline expands to show levels 1, 2, and 3.
7 Choose **File**, **Exit**	To close the document and Word.

Building slides from Word outlines

Explanation

When you create slides from a Word outline, a new slide is created for each level-1 heading in the outline. On each slide, the level-1 heading becomes the title, the level-2 heading becomes the first-level bullet, the level-3 heading becomes the second-level bullet, and so on. This feature helps you save time by creating the presentation from a Word outline rather than creating it from scratch in PowerPoint.

To create slides based on a Word outline:
1. Choose Insert, Slides From Outline.
2. Select the Word file that contains the outline.
3. Click the Insert button.

Do it!

B-2: Building slides from a Word outline

Here's how	Here's why
1 Maximize PowerPoint	On the taskbar, click the Microsoft Office PowerPoint button.
Select the third slide	If necessary.
2 Choose **Insert**, **Slides from Outline...**	To open the Insert Outline dialog box.
3 Select **Spices outline**	(From the current unit folder.) This Word file contains an outline for three new slides.
Click **Insert**	To create the new slides based on the selected Word file.
4 Scroll through the presentation	Three new slides have been added at the end of the presentation.
Observe the fourth slide	The level-1 heading was inserted as the title of the slide. The level-2 headings were inserted as the first-level bullet items.
Observe the fifth slide	The level-3 headings were inserted as second-level bullet items.
5 Update the presentation	

Inserting Word tables

Explanation

You can embed or link Word tables in a presentation in the same way you embed or link an Excel worksheet.

To insert a Word table into a presentation:

1 Choose Insert, Object to open the Insert Object dialog box.
2 Select Create from file, and then click the Browse button to open the Browse dialog box.
3 Select the Word file, and click OK.
4 If you want to link the table, check the Link check box. If you want to embed the table, clear the Link check box.
5 Click OK.

Do it!

B-3: Inserting a Word table

Here's how	Here's why
1 Move to the fifth slide	(If necessary) You'll insert a Word table into this slide.
2 Delete all the items in the second-level bulleted list	
3 Choose **Insert, Object...**	To open the Insert Object dialog box.
4 Select **Create from file**	
Click **Browse**	To open the Browse dialog box.
5 Select **Requirement**	(From the current unit folder.) You'll insert a table from this Word document into the current slide.
Click **OK**	To close the Browse dialog box.
Check **Link**	To link the table.
Click **OK**	The slide now contains a table.
6 Right-click the table, and choose **Format Object...**	
Click the **Size** tab	
Verify that Lock aspect ratio is checked	To maintain the existing height-to-width ratio.

7   Under Scale, in the Height box, enter **150**

    Press TAB — The value in the Width box changes automatically.

    Click **OK**

8   Reposition the table on the slide as shown

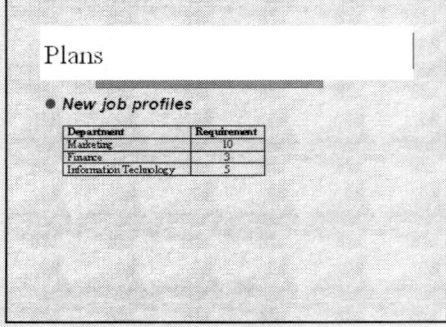

9   Double-click the table — The table opens in Word. You'll now edit the table.

10 In the table, change Requirement for Finance to **5**

11 Save and close the document

    Choose **File**, **Exit** — To close Word.

    Maximize PowerPoint — (If necessary.) Notice that the change is reflected in the table in PowerPoint as well.

12 Update the presentation

Sending and editing presentations in Word

Explanation

You might want to create a summary of your presentation that includes slide numbers, small-scale versions of each slide, and all accompanying speaker notes. To do this, you can send your presentation to Word. Just as you import an Excel worksheet into a PowerPoint presentation by linking or embedding it, you can link or embed PowerPoint slides in a Word document.

If you embed the slides in a Word document, the slides are saved as part of the Word file. As a result, any changes made in the slides in Word will not be reflected in the PowerPoint source file, and vice versa.

If you link the slides, then double-clicking a slide in Word will automatically open the slide in PowerPoint, and any changes made will be reflected in both PowerPoint and Word. Furthermore, if you modify the source PowerPoint file while the linked Word file is closed, the slides in the Word file will update automatically the next time you open it.

To send a PowerPoint presentation to Word:

1. Choose File, Send To, Microsoft Office Word to open the Send To Microsoft Word dialog box, shown in Exhibit 7-3.
2. Under Page layout in Microsoft Word, select a page layout of your choice.
3. Under Add slides to Microsoft Word document, select Paste if you want to embed the slides in the Word document. Select Paste link if you want to link the slides.
4. Click OK.

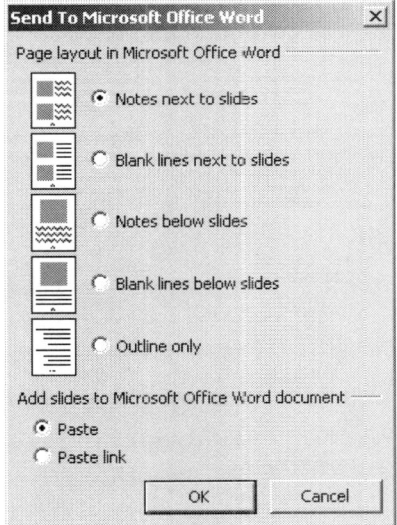

Exhibit 7-3: The Send To Microsoft Word dialog box

The following table explains the various options in the Send To Microsoft Word dialog box:

Option	Description
Notes next to slides	Places each slide's notes next to the slide, on the right, in the Microsoft Word document.
Blank lines next to slides	Places blank lines to the right of each slide in the Microsoft Word document.
Notes below slides	Places each slide's notes under the slide in the Microsoft Word document.
Blank lines below slides	Places blank lines under each slide in the Microsoft Word document.
Outline only	Creates an outline of the entire presentation in the Microsoft Word document.
Paste	Embeds your slides in the Microsoft Word document. There's no link between the source presentation file and the destination Word document. You can double-click the slides in the Word document to use PowerPoint to edit them.
Paste link	Inserts your slide in the Microsoft Word document and creates a link between the source presentation file and the destination Word document. The slides are updated each time you open the Word document and whenever the presentation changes.

Microsoft Office integration

Do it!

B-4: Sending a presentation to Word and editing it

Here's how	Here's why
1 Choose **File**, **Send To**, **Microsoft Office Word...**	To open the Send To Microsoft Office Word dialog box.
2 Select **Blank lines next to slides**	To create blank lines next to each slide in the Word document.
Under Add slides to Microsoft Office Word document, verify that Paste is selected	To ensure that the slides will be embedded (rather than linked) in the Word document. This means that any changes you make in the slides in Word will not be reflected in the PowerPoint file source, and vice versa.
Click **OK**	To send the slides to Word.
3 Scroll through the document	A table is created in which each slide is accompanied by a slide number and a set of blank lines.
4 Double-click the fourth slide	You'll edit the text in this slide.
5 Edit the title to read **Phase Two status**	To make this title consistent with the title of the presentation. Remember that because you embedded the slides, this change will not affect the source file.
6 Deselect the slide	
7 Save the document as **My Overview**	(In the current unit folder.) Choose File, Save As.
Close the document	Do not close Word.
8 Maximize PowerPoint	
Move to the fourth slide	The title of the fourth slide hasn't change.
9 Update and close the presentation	

Creating RTF outlines

Explanation

Rich Text Format (RTF) is a file format that supports text formatting, bullets, and alignment. Similar to creating a presentation based on a Word outline, you can save a presentation as an RTF outline. You can then open the RTF file in Word to see the outline. An RTF file converts all the formatting in a document to standard instructions so that the file can be opened in any Microsoft or Microsoft-compatible application. (However, graphics are not included in this format.)

To create an RTF outline:

1. Choose File, Save As to open the Save As dialog box.
2. From the Save as type list, select Outline/RTF.
3. Click OK.

Do it!

B-5: Saving a presentation as an RTF outline

Here's how	Here's why
1 Open Presentation	(From the current unit folder.) You will save the presentation as an RTF file, but this file format will not include any graphics used on the slides.
2 Choose **File, Save As...**	
3 From the Save as type list, select **Outline/RTF**	(Scroll down, if necessary.) You'll save the presentation as an RTF outline.
Click **Save**	Graphics and tables are not included in the RTF file format.
4 Maximize Word	
5 Open Presentation	To view the RTF outline. Without the graphics, it's difficult to identify the individual slides.
6 Choose **File, Exit**	To close Word.
Maximize PowerPoint	If necessary.
7 Close Presentation	

Unit summary: Microsoft Office integration

Topic A In this topic, you learned how to **import an Excel worksheet** into a PowerPoint presentation by **linking** or **embedding** the worksheet. Then, you learned how to **edit** the values in an embedded Excel worksheet. You also learned how to change the **background fill color** and **line style** of the worksheet.

Topic B In this topic, you learned how to create slides automatically based on a **Word outline**. You also learned how to **insert** a **Word table** in a presentation, **send a presentation to Word**, **edit** a presentation in Word, and save a presentation as an **RTF outline**.

Independent practice activity

1 Create a new, blank presentation.
2 Select the Title and Content layout.
3 Type **Employee data** as the slide title.
4 Embed the Excel file named Employee data (from the current unit folder).
5 Edit cell C7 to read **1466 8th Street**, and edit cell F7 to read **503-325-3071**.
6 Apply bold formatting to the column headings, and change the color to a color of your choice.
7 Using the Word outline named Employee details (from the current unit folder), add three new slides to the end of the presentation.
8 Send the presentation to Word (embed the slides with blank lines below the slide).
9 In Word, edit the title of the fourth slide to read **Database**.
10 Close Word without saving changes.
11 Save the presentation as **My practice employee data** and close it.
12 Close PowerPoint.

Review questions

1 When you import an object from one application into another, two files are involved. What are these files called?

2 When you make any changes in an embedded worksheet, they are reflected in the source file. True or False?

3 List the steps used to create slides from a Word outline.

4 You can embed or link Word tables in a presentation in the same way you embed or link an Excel worksheet. True or False?

5 List the steps used to send a PowerPoint presentation to Word.

Appendix A

Microsoft Office Specialist exam objectives map

This appendix provides the following information:

A Exam objectives for PowerPoint 2003 and references to corresponding material in Course ILT courseware.

Topic A: Comprehensive exam objectives

Explanation The following table lists the Microsoft Office Specialist exam objectives for PowerPoint 2003 and provides a reference to the location of both the conceptual material and the activities that teach each objective.

Objective	Course level	Conceptual information	Supporting activities
Creating presentations using automated tools (e.g., AutoContent Wizard)	Basic	Unit 2, Topic A, p 11	A-4
Creating presentations using templates	Basic	Unit 7, Topic A, p 2	A-1
Adding text to and deleting text from slides	Basic	Unit 2, Topic A, pp 5-9	A-2, A-3
Checking spelling and grammar	Basic	Unit 8 Topic A, p 2	A-1
Checking usage (e.g., Thesaurus)	Basic	Unit 8 Topic A, p 7	A-3
Importing text from other sources	Advanced	Unit 7, Topic A, p 2 Unit 7, Topic B, p 9-10	A-1 B-2
Creating tables, charts and diagrams	Basic	Unit 6, Topic A, p 2 Unit 6, Topic B, p 7 Unit 6, Topic C, pp 19-20	A-1 B-1 C-1
Adding pictures, shapes and other graphics to slides (e.g., ClipArt, AutoShapes, WordArt)	Basic	Unit 4, Topic A, p 2 Unit 4, Topic B, p 12 Unit 5, Topic A, p 2 Unit 5, Topic B, p 7 Unit 5, Topic C, p 11	A-1 B-1 A-1 B-1 C-1
Inserting objects (e.g., Excel charts, media clips, Paintbrush pictures)	Basic	Unit 6, Topic B, p 13 Unit 5, Topic C, p 10	B-3 C-1
	Advanced	Unit 2, Topic B, pp 10-12	B-1, B-2
Modifying font typeface, style, color and size	Basic	Unit 3, Topic A, pp 2-4	A-1, A-2
Aligning text	Basic	Unit 3, Topic C, p 23	C-3
Changing the size and color of pictures, shapes and other graphics	Basic	Unit 4, Topic A, p 7 Unit 4, Topic B, p 14 Unit 4, Topic D, p 24 Unit 5, Topic A, p 2	A-3 B-2 D-1 A-1
Aligning, connecting and rotating pictures, shapes and other graphics	Basic	Unit 4, Topic A, p 10	A-5
	Advanced	Unit 2, Topic A, p 8	A-3
Adding effects to pictures, shapes and other graphics	Basic	Unit 5, Topic C, pp 13-14	C-2, C-3
	Advanced	Unit 2, Topic A, p 5	A-2

Objective	Course level	Conceptual information	Supporting activities
Customizing slide backgrounds	Advanced	Unit 1, Topic B, p 4	B-1
Modifying slide layout	Basic	Unit 2, Topic A, p 6	A-3
Applying design templates	Basic	Unit 7, Topic A, p 4	A-1
Modifying page setup	Basic	Unit 8, Topic C, p 13	C-2
Applying an animation scheme to a single slide, group of slides, or an entire presentation	Advanced	Unit 2, Topic C, p 16	C-3
Applying transition effects to a single slide, group of slides, or an entire presentation	Basic	Unit 7, Topic C, pp 16-19	C-1, C-2, C-3
Customizing templates	Advanced	Unit 1, Topic A, p 2	A-1
Inserting content in headers and footers	Basic	Unit 7, Topic D, pp 26-28	D-2, D-3
	Advanced	Unit 1, Topic C, pp 8-10	C-1, C-2
Creating and managing multiple masters	Basic	Unit 7, Topic B, pp 11-15	B-4, B-5, B-6
Adding, deleting and modifying placeholders	Basic	Unit 2, Topic A, p 6-7	A-3
Tracking, accepting, and rejecting changes in a presentation	Advanced	Unit 4, Topic C, p 12	C-3
Adding, editing and deleting comments in a presentation	Advanced	Unit 4, Topic C, p 11	C-2
Comparing and merging presentations	Advanced	Unit 4, Topic C, p 12	C-3
Adding, deleting and rearranging slides	Basic	Unit 2, Topic A, p 6 Unit 2, Topic D, pp 21-24 Unit 2, Topic E, p 25	A-3 D-1, D-2, D-3 E-1
Using normal, slide sorter, note pages and zoom views	Basic	Unit 1, Topic A, p 8 Unit 7, Topic D, p 24	A-3 D-1
Adding hyperlinks to slides	Basic	Unit 8, Topic D, pp 22-24	D-2, D-3
Setting grids and guides	Basic	Unit 4, Topic B, p 15	B-3
Creating and editing custom shows	Advanced	Unit 4, Topic B, pp 6-7	B-1, B-2
Adding and modifying Action buttons	Advanced	Unit 4, Topic A, pp 2-5	A-1, A-2
Hiding slides	Basic	Unit 8, Topic B, p 11	B-2
Rehearsing and saving timing of presentations	Basic	Unit 7, Topic C, p 22	C-5

Objective	Course level	Conceptual information	Supporting activities
Navigating presentations in Slide Show view	Basic	Unit 1, Topic A, pp 2-3	A-1
Using pens, highlighters, arrows and pointers for emphasis	Advanced	Unit 5, Topic D, p 16	D-2
Packaging presentations to folders for storage on a Compact Disc (e.g., Package for CD)	Advanced	Unit 5, Topic C, p 13	C-3
Scheduling and defining settings for Online Broadcasts	Advanced	Unit 5, Topic A, p 3	A-2
Creating and using folders for presentation storage	Basic	Unit 2, Topic B, pp 13-15	B-1, B-2
	Advanced	Unit 5, Topic C, p 13	C-3
Saving slides in different folders and with different file names	Basic	Unit 2, Topic B, pp 13-15	B-1, B-2
Saving presentations as Web pages	Basic	Unit 8, Topic D, pp 20-21	D-1
Publishing slides and presentations as Web pages and setting publishing options	Basic	Unit 8, Topic D, pp 20-21	D-1
Printing slides, outlines, handouts and speaker notes	Basic	Unit 8, Topic C, p 17-18	C-5
Previewing slides for printing and changing preview options	Basic	Unit 8, Topic C, p 12	C-1
Modifying printing options	Basic	Unit 8, Topic C, pp 17-18	C-4, C-5
Sending presentations to Microsoft Word	Advanced	Unit 7, Topic B, pp 12-13	B-4

Course summary

This summary contains information to help you bring the course to a successful conclusion. Using this information, you will be able to:

A Use the summary text to reinforce what you've learned in class.

B Determine the next courses in this series (if any), as well as any other resources that might help you continue to learn about PowerPoint 2003.

Topic A: Course summary

Use the following summary text to reinforce what you've learned in class.

Unit summaries

Unit 1

In this unit, you learned how to **modify** a template in **Slide Master view**. You also learned how to build a **custom template** from a blank presentation and how to build a **custom slide master**, to which you added a **symbol** and a **WordArt object**. Finally, you learned how to maintain **multiple slide masters** in a presentation.

Unit 2

In this unit, you learned how to modify clip art objects by **cropping** and **recoloring** them. Then you learned how to **add a background fill** and **apply a line style** to a clip art object. Next, you learned how to **rotate** an object. You also learned how to add **movie and sound clips** by using the **Clip Organizer**. Finally, you learned how to add **animation effects** and **scanned images** to a presentation.

Unit 3

In this unit, you learned how to **format an organization chart** by changing the chart layout, formatting text, adding border styles, and modifying the background color. Then, you learned how to **format and align text in a table**. You also learned how to **draw a table** by using the **Tables and Borders toolbar**.

Unit 4

In this unit, you learned how to **add** and **modify action buttons** in a presentation. You also learned how to **create** and **edit a custom slide show**. Finally, you learned how to **set up a review cycle**.

Unit 5

In this unit, you learned about using **Microsoft NetMeeting** to broadcast a **presentation on demand**. Next, you learned about the **Shared Workspace task pane**, and you learned how to **create a Document Workspace**. You also learned how to **embed fonts** and **compress pictures** in a presentation. Then, you learned how to **package a presentation** by using the **Package for CD feature** and how to **run** the presentation. Finally, you learned how to use **on-screen navigation tools** and **annotate a slide**.

Unit 6

In this unit, you learned how to **customize** and **create toolbars**. You also learned how to automate complex tasks by **creating and running a macro**.

Unit 7

In this unit, you learned how to **embed** an **Excel worksheet** in a presentation. You also learned how to **edit** and **format** an embedded worksheet. Next, you learned how to **build slides from a Word outline**. Then, you learned how to **insert a Word table** in a presentation, **send a presentation to Word,** and **edit a PowerPoint presentation in Word**. Finally, you learned how to **save a presentation as an RTF outline**.

Topic B: Continued learning after class

It is impossible to learn to use any software effectively in a single day. To get the most out of this class, you should begin working with Microsoft PowerPoint 2003 to perform real tasks as soon as possible. Course Technology also offers resources for continued learning.

Next courses in this series

This is the last course in this series.

Other resources

For more information, visit www.course.com.

PowerPoint 2003: Advanced
Quick reference

Button	Shortcut keys	Function
B	CTRL + B	Makes selected text bold.
I	CTRL + I	Italicizes selected text.
U	CTRL + U	Underlines selected text.
S		Applies a shadow effect to selected text.
≡	CTRL + L	Left-aligns selected text.
≡	CTRL + E	Centers selected text.
≡	CTRL + R	Right-aligns selected text.
A˄	CTRL + SHIFT + >	Increases the font size of selected text.
		Inserts a new title master.
		Preserves a master.
		Renames a master.
▦		Opens Slide Sorter view.
🖥	SHIFT + F5	Runs a slide show from the current slide.
⊹		Activates the picture cropping tool.

Button	Shortcut keys	Function
		Opens the WordArt Gallery dialog box.
		On the WordArt toolbar, opens the Format WordArt dialog box. On the Picture toolbar, opens the Format Picture dialog box.
		Opens the Recolor Picture dialog box.
		Applies a line style.
		Applies a border around a table.
		Draws a table.
		Applies a border color to a table.
		Opens the Organization Chart Style Gallery.
		Opens the Compress Pictures dialog box.
	CTRL + D	Duplicates the selected object.
	DELETE	Clears or deletes the selected object.
		Displays the Slide Design task pane.
		Inserts a picture from a file.
		Stops a macro recording.

Glossary

action button
A navigation tool added to a slide to help viewers move through a presentation.

administrator
A Document Workspace role with full control over the workspace.

clip art
Pre-designed pictures, animations, sounds, and movies that you can insert into PowerPoint slides to give a presentation more impact.

Clip Organizer
Categorizes movie and sound clips into various collections, making them easier to locate and use.

contributor
A Document Workspace role with permission to add content to the existing documents in the workspace.

destination file
The target file when importing an object from one application into another.

Document Workspace Site
A SharePoint Services site that helps you share documents and information, such as task assignments and deadlines.

Format Painter
A tool available on the Standard toolbar, used to copy formatting attributes from one object to another.

Gallery tab
Located in the Revisions pane, this tab displays slides with changes made by reviewers. The name of the reviewer appears above each slide.

GIF
A standard image format used on the Web.

JPEG
A standard image format used on the Web.

List tab
Located in the Revisions pane, this tab displays all the changes and comments for a reviewed presentation. The list is color coded to distinguish between the changes made by different reviewers.

macro
A series of commands that you can execute automatically with a single command.

Meeting Workspace Site
A SharePoint Services site that helps you conduct online meetings and track the attendees, agenda, and decisions made in those meetings.

Microsoft NetMeeting
A feature that helps you interact with your viewers on multiple computers in different locations.

motion clips
PowerPoint's built-in movie clips. These clips are organized into various collections in the Clip Organizer.

organization chart
Displays hierarchical details, as in a company's personnel structure.

reader
A Document Workspace role with permission to read the documents in the workspace.

resolution
The number of dots per inch (dpi) that make up a picture or image.

review cycle
Involves four main steps: sending a presentation for review, reviewing a presentation, accepting or rejecting changes, and ending a review.

Rich Text Format (RTF)
A file format that supports text formatting, bullets, and alignment.

Shared Workspace
A Microsoft Windows SharePoint Services site where members of a team can share documents and exchange information about their projects.

Source file
The file of origin when importing an object from one application into another.

template
A presentation file that contains pre-designed formats and color schemes giving a presentation a consistent look. Templates are saved with the .pot file extension.

Web designer
A Document Workspace role with permission to create lists and document libraries and to customize pages in the Web site.

Index

A

Action buttons
   Adding, 4-2
   Modifying, 4-5
   With sound, 4-3
Animation
   Animating objects, 2-12
   Animating slides, 2-16
   Organizing effects, 2-14

C

Clip art
   Changing colors in, 2-5
   Cropping, 2-2
   Defined, 2-2
   Formatting, 2-5
   Rotating, 2-8
Clip Organizer, 2-10, 2-11, 2-19

D

Destination file, 7-2
Document Workspace
   Creating, 5-8
   Member roles, 5-5

E

Excel worksheets
   Editing, 7-6
   Embedding, 7-2
   Formatting, 7-6
   Inserting, 7-2
   Linking, 7-2

F

Fonts, embedding, 5-10
Footers
   Adding objects to, 1-10
   Adding symbols to, 1-8
Format Picture dialog box, 2-5

G

Graphics, adding to templates, 1-6

I

Images
   Adding scanned images, 2-17
   File formats, 2-17

M

Macros
   Creating, 6-8
   Defined, 6-8, 6-12
   Running, 6-10
Movie clips, adding, 2-10

N

NetMeeting, using to broadcast presentations, 5-2

O

Objects
   Animating, 2-12
   Rotating, 2-8
Organization charts
   Adding background colors to, 3-6, 3-18
   Adding border styles to, 3-6
   Applying styles to, 3-2
   Default styles for, 3-8
   Formatting text in, 3-4

P

Package for CD feature, 5-10, 5-14, 5-21
Pen tools, 5-18
Picture toolbar, 2-2, 2-5
Pictures, compressing, 5-12
Presentations
   Annotating, 5-18
   Broadcasting, 5-2
   Embedding fonts in, 5-10
   Inserting Excel sheets into, 7-2
   Inserting Word tables into, 7-11, 7-18
   Packaging, 5-14, 5-21
   Reviewing, 4-10
   Saving as RTF files, 7-16
   Sending out for review, 4-8
   Sending to Microsoft Word, 7-13

R

Review cycle
   Accepting or rejecting changes, 4-11
   Described, 4-8
   Reviewing a presentation, 4-10
   Starting, 4-8
Reviewers' comments, printing, 4-11
Reviewing toolbar, 4-10, 4-14

Revisions Pane, 4-11, 4-14
RTF outlines, creating, 7-16

S

Scanned images, adding, 2-17
Shared workspace
    Defined, 5-5
    Using, 5-5
Shared Workspace task pane, 5-5, 5-6, 5-8
Show Popup menu, 5-16
Slide masters
    Applying to selected slides, 1-16
    Duplicating, 1-13
    Editing, 1-14
    Renaming, 1-17
Slide shows
    Creating custom, 4-6
    Editing, 4-7
    Navigating with on-screen tools, 5-16
Slides
    Animating, 2-16
    Annotating, 5-18
    Building from Word outlines, 7-10
    Navigating through, 5-16
Sound clips, adding, 2-11
Source file, 7-2
Symbols, adding to footers, 1-8

T

Tables
    Drawing, 3-12
    Formatting, 3-9, 3-18
    Formatting text in, 3-10
    Inserting Word tables, 7-11, 7-18
Tables and Borders toolbar, 3-9, 3-12, 3-18
Templates
    Adding graphics to, 1-6
    Creating from blank presentations, 1-4
    Modifying, 1-2
Toolbars
    Creating, 6-5
    Customizing, 6-2
    Picture, 2-2, 2-5
    Reviewing, 4-10, 4-14
    Tables and Borders, 3-9, 3-12, 3-18

W

Word
    Inserting tables into presentations, 7-11, 7-18
    Outlines, 7-8
    Sending a presentation to, 7-13
WordArt, using in footers, 1-10